CLEOPATRA
and ANCIENT EGYPT
FOR KIDS

Her Life and World, with 21 Activities

SIMONETTA CARR

CHICAGO REVIEW PRESS

Copyright © 2018 by Simonetta Carr
All rights reserved
Published by Chicago Review Press Incorporated
814 North Franklin Street
Chicago, Illinois 60610
ISBN 978-1-61373-975-4

Library of Congress Cataloging-in-Publication Data

Names: Carr, Simonetta, author.
Title: Cleopatra and ancient Egypt for kids : her life and world, with 21
  activities / Simonetta Carr.
Description: Chicago, Illinois : Chicago Review Press Incorporated, 2018. |
  Includes bibliographical references and index. | Audience: Age 9–up. |
  Audience: Grade 4 to 6. |
Identifiers: LCCN 2017053333 (print) | LCCN 2017054371 (ebook) | ISBN
  9781613739761 (adobe pdf) | ISBN 9781613739778 (kindle) | ISBN
  9781613739785 (epub) | ISBN 9781613739754 (trade paper)
Subjects: LCSH: Cleopatra, Queen of Egypt, –30 B.C.—Juvenile literature. |
  Queens—Egypt—Biography—Juvenile literature. | Egypt—Kings and
  rulers—Biography—Juvenile literature. | Egypt—History—332–30
  B.C.—Juvenile literature.
Classification: LCC DT92.7 (ebook) | LCC DT92.7 .C38 2018 (print) | DDC
  932/.021092 [B] —dc23
LC record available at https://lccn.loc.gov/2017053333

Cover and interior design: Sarah Olson
Cover images: Painting from the tomb of Nebaum: Erich Lessing/Art
Resource, NY; Bust of Cleopatra: bpk Bildagentur/Antikensammlung,
Staatliche Museen, Berlin, Germany/Johannes Laurentius/Art Resource,
NY; Coins: Wikimedia Commons; Model of river boat: The Walters Art
Museum, Baltimore; Bust of Mark Antony: Alinari/Art Resource, NY;
Nile Oasis: Jose Ignacio Soto/123rf.com; Pyramids of Giza: Wikimedia
Commons; Statue of Cleopatra VII: DeA Picture Library/Art Resource,
NY; Temple of Hathor: David Lewis/Flickr; Servants plucking geese: Erich
Lessing/Art Resource, NY
Back cover images: Mummy case; Tablet with Isis, Horus, and Ram; and
Scarab from Egyptian-style necklace: The Walters Art Museum, Baltimore;
Game board: Musée de Mariemont/Wikimedia Commons
Illustrations: Lindsey Cleworth Schauer
Map design: Chris Erichsen

Printed in the United States of America
5 4 3 2 1

To my critical-thinking family and all
those who love discovering what might
lie behind popular stories

CONTENTS

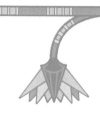

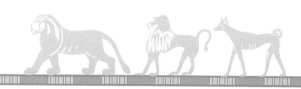

NOTE TO READERS

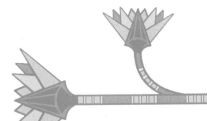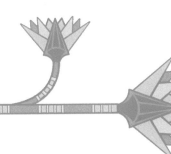

The 3,000-year-long Egyptian civilization—one of the most refined and longest-lasting of the ancient world—has left a significant and enduring impact on history. Many volumes have been written on this subject, which continues to intrigue and fascinate.

This book looks back at ancient Egypt from its twilight—the time when Cleopatra VII was queen. In spite of her attempts to keep her family on the throne, her death marked the end of the Egyptian **dynasties** (ruling families) and, for all practical purposes, the beginning of the Roman Empire. As you follow her adventurous story, you will see Egyptian history and culture as she might have seen it—a history and culture she greatly admired and respected.

You will encounter the most important Egyptian monuments and works of art, observe how Egyptians lived and overcame their greatest challenges, explore some reasons for the collapse of such an impressive empire, and learn how Egyptian culture and discoveries have affected our world.

The maps and time lines will assist you in this quest. The activities will help you step back in time and experience, for example, how Egyptians transported heavy **obelisks** (a type of pillar) and watered fields, or how Cleopatra might have made a pearl disappear. They will also give you a better appreciation of Egyptian art and poetry.

There is of course much more to learn about Cleopatra and the remarkable Egyptian civilization than what's in these pages. I hope this book will be a springboard to greater learning. If you're interested in discovering more, be sure to check out "Resources to Explore" on page 121.

TIME LINE

All dates are BC, so the numbers decrease as the time gets closer to year 0. Keep this in mind as you read the book.

70 OR 69 | Cleopatra VII is born during the winter, probably in Alexandria, Egypt

58 | Cleopatra's father, King Ptolemy XII, flees Egypt to Rome

Berenice IV, Cleopatra's older sister, is appointed queen in his place

55 | Ptolemy XII is restored to the throne

Berenice is killed

51 | Ptolemy XII dies a natural death

Cleopatra and her brother Ptolemy XIII become rulers of Egypt

49 | In Rome, a civil war between Julius Caesar and Gnaeus Pompey begins

48 | Cleopatra flees Egypt

Pompey is killed in Egypt

Caesar's arrival marks the beginning of the Alexandrian War

Cleopatra's sister Arsinoe IV rules Egypt briefly

Ptolemy XIII is defeated and killed, and Caesar installs Cleopatra and her youngest brother, Ptolemy XIV, as rulers of Egypt

47 | Cleopatra has a son and names him Ptolemy XV Caesar Theos Philopator Philometor (nicknamed Caesarion)

46 | In Rome, Caesar celebrates his victories

Cleopatra and Ptolemy XIV visit Rome to receive formal recognition

44 | Caesar is killed

Cleopatra, probably on her second visit to Rome, returns to Egypt, where Ptolemy XIV dies

Cleopatra rules Egypt with her son Caesarion

41 | The Roman consul Mark Antony meets Cleopatra in Tarsus, and they spend the winter together in Alexandria

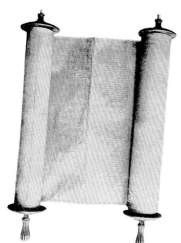

INTRODUCTION

THE ENDLESS SEARCH FOR THE TRUE CLEOPATRA

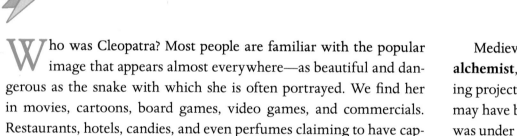

Who was Cleopatra? Most people are familiar with the popular image that appears almost everywhere—as beautiful and dangerous as the snake with which she is often portrayed. We find her in movies, cartoons, board games, video games, and commercials. Restaurants, hotels, candies, and even perfumes claiming to have captured the secret ingredient that brought two powerful men to her feet have all adopted her name as a trademark.

Cleopatra's image has varied from century to century and from place to place, usually to fit people's motives and expectations. The Romans, eager to save the reputations of two of their most renowned generals, represented her as cunning and essentially irresistible. Over the course of centuries, her tragic love story has overshadowed other aspects of her life. It was the main focus of Shakespeare's heartrending tragedy *Antony and Cleopatra* and was later echoed in many romantic and glamorous movies.

Medieval Arab **scholars** instead regarded her as a brilliant scientist, **alchemist**, and philosopher and praised her for her magnificent building projects. Since most of these men were Egyptian, their comments may have been an expression of national pride. Likewise, while Egypt was under British colonial rule (1882–1914), Cleopatra's death took on a deeper meaning as the ultimate expression of love and national struggle for freedom.

Today, a growing appreciation of women's contributions to history has recast Cleopatra as an intelligent and fiercely independent ruler who courageously took on the throne at a young age, escaped death at the hands of her violent family, and held her place in one of the most crucial times of history, standing up to Rome's unconquerable world power.

Are any of these views correct? Is the truth a mixture of them? Many books claim to tell Cleopatra's true story, but can anyone be certain which one is correct? **Archaeological** evidence is still scarce.

There are no documents written by her and few by those closest to her. Even her date of birth is based on just one uncertain account. But what little is available offers food for thought to anyone who is willing to leave behind common notions and personal preferences.

A lot of fun is in the discovery. Did she really meet Caesar by hiding in a rolled-up carpet? Did she die by snakebite? How was she able to keep her country stable when, in effect, its days of independence were numbered? Why did the people of Rome hate her? Was she really as evil as they described her? Why did her image change so much throughout history, and why does she still capture the interest and imagination of artists and writers?

This book will explore these questions and many others, offering some possible answers and allowing you to draw your own conclusions. You will follow Cleopatra from her childhood to her death, through many dangers, adventures, travels, epic decisions, and unexpected outcomes. You will also meet some of the most important people of her time and see how her story fits into the dramatic transition from one monumental era to another.

A Young Princess
of an Ancient Land

There was sweetness also in the tones of her voice; and her tongue, like an instrument of many strings, she could readily turn to whatever language she pleased. —Plutarch

During the winter of 70 BC, in the ancient land of Egypt, a princess was born. She was called Cleopatra, a Greek name that had already graced other powerful royal women in her family. It had a promising meaning: "her father's fame."

This sounds like the beginning of a beautiful fairy tale. In reality, life for a **pharaoh**'s daughter was marked by uncertainty and frequent threats to her life. Power was a highly desired prize and could move anyone, even a member of her own family, to go to any length to obtain it.

Temple of Hathor at Dendera, on the west bank of the Nile. *David Lewis, Flickr*

A Greek Family on the Throne of Egypt

Gruesome murders and puzzling mysteries already stained Cleopatra's family history. The Ptolemies were a tough and ambitious clan from the rough, mountainous region of Macedonia, in northern Greece. In nearly 300 years of their rule over Egypt, they had often proven themselves ruthless and cold blooded against both enemies and potential enemies—relatives included.

To understand how a Greek family ended up on the Egyptian throne, one must go back to the year 323 BC, when Alexander the Great, the most powerful Greek ruler, died unexpectedly at the peak of his conquests, apparently using his last breath to bestow his massive empire on "the strongest." These words gave way to fierce power struggles. In the end, his territories were split among his generals, ending his dream of a universal empire.

A general named Ptolemy took over Egypt and rose to its throne as Ptolemy I Soter (Savior). He also hijacked Alexander's funeral procession, stole his body, and brought it to the city Alexander had built on the Mediterranean coast of Egypt: Alexandria. This is the city where, about 350 years later, Cleopatra was born.

Groomed for the Crown

Cleopatra's Alexandria was a thriving metropolis. Thanks to the Ptolemies, it had become one of the most outstanding cities in the Mediterranean world—both as an active port and as a center of learning. It was also blatantly Greek, filled as it was with a large Greek population and a great number of Greek structures and facilities, such as an outdoor theater for staging Greek plays; an open square called an **agora**, where people could buy goods and hear different speakers; and a gymnasium where men could practice sports, compete, and attend cultural events.

Cleopatra lived in the royal palaces with her family: her father, Ptolemy XII; her older sister, Berenice; her younger sister, Arsinoe; and two brothers, both called Ptolemy. Ptolemy XII's wife, Cleopatra V, died sometime during his reign, so

This mosaic from Pompeii, Italy, circa 80 BC, depicts Alexander the Great during the Battle of Issus.
Scala / Art Resource, NY

2

THE PEOPLE OF ALEXANDRIA

Alexandria was mostly composed of three groups of people who lived in separate parts of town. The Greeks, who had the most privileged status and usually the best jobs, had first come to Alexandria with prospects of starting profitable enterprises. They were the most vocal opponents of the Ptolemies' alliance with Rome.

The first Egyptians who moved to Alexandria, instead, moved there reluctantly to perform much-needed construction work and other forms of common labor. These social distinctions between Greeks and Egyptians remained, although some educated and wealthy Egyptians were able to attain good positions in the capital, as long as they could speak Greek.

The third group was composed of Jews, who had come to Egypt at different times to escape unfavorable conditions at home (approximately in the region of modern Israel). While many Jews eventually returned to their country, many others decided to stay, especially in Alexandria, which ended up hosting the biggest Jewish population outside the Roman **province** of Judaea. Many Jews worked as administrators, **scribes** who wrote out and copied documents, and **mercenary** soldiers paid to fight on behalf of Egypt.

The three groups kept mostly to themselves, observing their own customs and worshiping in their separate temples. The Greeks lived in the city center, the Jews in the eastern part of town, and the Egyptians in the western area. Ptolemy I tried to intertwine the Greek and Egyptian religions by promoting the cult of Serapis, a combination of the Egyptian god Osiris and a group of Greek gods, as a new god for a new world, but few Egyptians warmed to this idea. The Jews remained mostly faithful to their one god, Adonai.

A statue of the god Serapis from his temple at Alexandria. Serapis, who was represented as either a bull or a Greek hero, became famous all over the Hellenistic (Greek) world but was not popular among the Egyptians, who preferred their traditional gods. *The Walters Art Museum, Baltimore*

CREATE A WRITING TABLET

*In ancient times, people used wax tablets for writings that didn't have to be preserved for a long time (for example, for notes or first drafts, which were later copied on **papyrus** sheets or **parchment**—both expensive materials). A plaster tablet written by a schoolboy in Thebes is now in the British Museum in London. Pieces of broken pots (called* ostraka*) were also utilized as "scrap paper."*

Make your own writing tablet using modeling clay instead of wax or plaster.

MATERIALS

- 5-by-7-inch picture frame with securely fastening cardboard backing
- ½ pound nonhardening modeling clay
- Rolling pin
- Plastic modeling tools

1. Remove the glass and any paper (such as a stock photo, decorative pattern, or brand name) from the picture frame by first removing the cardboard backing. Return the cardboard backing to the frame, securing with the fasteners provided.

2. Knead the modeling clay until it's soft enough to be flattened.

3. Using a rolling pin, flatten the clay until it is about ¼ inch thick.

4. Carefully place the flattened clay over the cardboard backing inside the frame.

5. Using a sharp plastic modeling tool, cut excess modeling clay away from the frame so that the frame is fully visible around the clay but the cardboard is hidden.

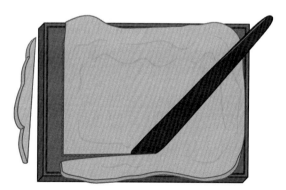

6. Use a pointed modeling tool to write your message.

7. To erase what you have written, use a flat modeling tool or your fingers to smooth the clay.

it's not clear if she was the mother of all these children or if Ptolemy XII remarried. They might also have had another daughter, Cleopatra VI. The Cleopatra in this story is known as Cleopatra VII.

The royal palaces were located in a very private northeastern section of Alexandria generally known as "the Palaces"—essentially a city within Alexandria that had grown to occupy about one-third of Alexandria's total area.

The royal palaces were spacious—one-fifth of Alexandria's size—surrounded by flourishing gardens and connected by courtyards lined with columns. Inside, they were filled with beautiful and exotic objects from all parts of Egypt and other countries, each new item more splendid than the others, because each new Ptolemy tried to outdo his or her predecessors.

Cleopatra spent a rather peaceful childhood in Alexandria. In the Greek education system, children started school at age seven, when they were expected to put away childish toys and focus on their studies, and the Ptolemies might have followed the same rule.

Most girls in Cleopatra's time received only the basic instruction necessary to run a home. Things were different, however, in the Egyptian **court**, where queens played an essential role in running their country, whether as mothers, wives, or—when necessary—single rulers. For this reason, and because of the high value the Ptolemies placed on education, Cleopatra and her sisters had excellent tutors, comparable to those of their two younger brothers.

No one knows how long Cleopatra continued her formal studies, but she informally kept learning for the rest of her life. She certainly read and memorized the works of many ancient authors, especially Homer, who was then considered the greatest Greek poet of all time. According to some medieval Arab writers, she was also very interested in mathematics and science.

Alexandria was an ideal place for learning. Two buildings in the Palaces area, built by the first two Ptolemies, attracted scholars from all over the known world. One building was the Library of Alexandria, a library so large that, in Cleopatra's

Papyrus reeds like the ones in this picture were harvested and cut. After cutting out the outer layer of the stems, Egyptians cut the pith in thin slices, soaked it in water, hammered the pieces together, dried the resulting sheet under a weight, and polished it.
Samantha Chesler–Leiman, Flickr

MAKE AN ARCHIMEDES SCREW

*Archimedes, originally from Sicily, in Italy, was one of the scientists who worked in the Alexandrian Museum. He is most famous for discovering why some objects float in water and others sink, but he also created many useful inventions. One of the best-known devices attributed to him (even though it was already in use in simpler forms) is the Archimedes screw—a contraption adopted to raise water to higher ground. This tool was very important for field **irrigation** (watering) and ship draining.*

Originally these screws were made of wood and looked like huge versions of the common screws found in a hardware store. This activity uses plastic tubing and a bottle. The materials are different, but the principle is the same.

MATERIALS

- Plastic drop cloth
- 5 feet clear plastic tubing, ¼ inch wide
- 1-liter plastic or glass water bottle
- Duct tape (or other strong tape)
- Water
- Large mixing bowl
- Food coloring
- Cardboard spaghetti box (or similar-size box)
- Small bowl

1. Place the plastic drop cloth on the surface you are using (table, floor, etc.).

2. Hold one end of the tube against the side of a full water bottle at the bottle's bottom edge. The tube should be parallel to the bottle's bottom, with the end pointing out sideways. Use duct tape to secure the tube to the side of the bottle about ½ inch from the tube's end.

3. Wrap the tube around the bottle in a spiral, going counterclockwise, until the other end of the tube is just past the mouth of the bottle.

4. As with the first end, secure this end of the tube to the side of the bottle near the bottle's mouth, leaving about ½ inch of the tube free.

5. Add another piece of tape about halfway down the tube to secure it firmly to the bottle.

6. Pour water into a large mixing bowl until it is about ¾ full.

7. Add 3–5 drops of food coloring into the water and mix well.

8. Place a spaghetti box flat next to the large bowl. Then put a small, empty bowl on top of the box.

9. Place the bottom of the bottle in the large bowl so that the bottom end of the tube is in the water, and angle the bottle so that the top end of the tube is above the small bowl.

10. Slowly turn the bottle clockwise so that the bottom end of the tube scoops up the colored water.

11. Watch the water rise slowly through the tube until it pours into the small bowl.

12. Try turning the tube the opposite way. Does it work? Why not?

day, it held approximately 500,000 papyrus scrolls (the "books" of that time). Connected to it was an impressive building called the Alexandrian Museum. Unlike most of today's museums, this was not just a place to hold collections of interesting and valuable objects. It was a state-sponsored center of learning (unique for its time), where the best minds from all over the known world resided for some time to research and teach.

Generally speaking, the Ptolemies made no effort to learn the Egyptian language, or to teach it to their children. That's why the Greek biographer Plutarch, writing 100 years after Cleopatra's death, was particularly surprised that she could "pass from one language to another" so easily that she usually didn't need an interpreter. Besides Egyptian, she could speak the languages of the Ethiopians, Hebrews, Arabs, Syrians, Medes (who lived in a portion of today's Iraq), and Parthians (in today's Iraq and Iran).

Plutarch's statement is a testimony to Cleopatra's exceptional intelligence and love for learning. Her language skills might also say something about her political insight. For a ruler, speaking other languages—especially those of her people—inspires trust, promotes understanding, and opens doors.

Study and work didn't occupy all of the Ptolemies' time. They were famous for their long and extravagant banquets, which included costly

A papyrus scroll. *Internet Archive Book Images, from Frederic G. Kenyon, Our Bible and the Ancient Manuscripts: Being a History of the Text and Its Translations (1895), 41*

Cleopatra's father, Ptolemy XII Auletes.
© RMN-Grand Palais / Art Resource, NY

A BLACK CLEOPATRA?

No source from Cleopatra's time mentions her skin color, and some people have recently wondered if she had African ancestry. The possibility should not be excluded.

The Ptolemies were originally Macedonian, but it's difficult to determine their precise appearance in an age when intermarriages were common. Even if they traditionally married close relatives in order to keep the power in the family, at least some of them had secondary, unrecorded wives who could have been of different ethnicities, including African.

It's safe to assume that Cleopatra had dark hair and light- or medium-brown skin like the majority of people who lived in the nations around the Mediterranean. Even this, however, is only an assumption. In reality, no one knows for sure.

robes, elaborate decorations, and plenty of music, games, food, and especially wine—which might have been mixed with water, in typical Macedonian style.

Outside the palace, the Alexandrian calendar was filled with exciting occasions, including a major sports event (called Ptolemaia in honor of Ptolemy I) that rivaled the Olympic Games, and innumerable Egyptian and Greek religious festivals. These celebrations brought crowds to the streets and usually ended with outdoor banquets and public entertainment for all. Festivals in honor of Dionysus, the Greek god of wine, were especially magnificent during Cleopatra's youth, and her father, Ptolemy XII, loved to introduce himself as "the new Dionysus."

The citizens of Alexandria preferred to create their own nicknames for their kings. To them, Ptolemy XII was Auletes, "the flute player." It might have been a reference to the king's chubby cheeks. If he actually played a flute, the name would not have been a compliment, because playing musical instruments was not considered a proper activity for kings. In any case, they especially detested him for his strong ties to Rome, which they saw as a political threat and viewed as less cultured.

The High Cost of Security

If Roman culture was not yet a match to the sophisticated Greeks, it was the rising political superpower. Born as a small city-state in the mid-eighth century BC, Rome had already conquered a great number of nations and was still rapidly expanding.

As the Roman population grew, however, so did its need for provisions, especially grain (wheat and barley), since bread was the main staple food at that time. Though generally fertile, the small and mountainous Italian peninsula could not meet this increasing need. But across the Mediterranean Sea, Egypt, with its lengthy spread of fruitful fields around the Nile River, had the ability to exceed Rome's national demand.

Rome needed Egypt's fabulous riches, and the Ptolemies, plagued by outside threats and inside rebellions, needed Rome's protection. It might sound like a good match, if it weren't for Rome's great power, not only to protect but also to crush. The Ptolemies knew that in order to retain their rule of Egypt they'd have to keep Rome happy by any possible means, including great gifts. The most outrageous of these gifts was found in the last will of Cleopatra's great-uncle Ptolemy X, who died in 88 BC, leaving his whole kingdom (including Egypt and Cyprus) to Rome.

The Roman government didn't take this will too seriously. It was easier to let foreign rulers govern their regions under Rome's control than to take over a country's entire administration (and all of its problems). The will did provide a convenient

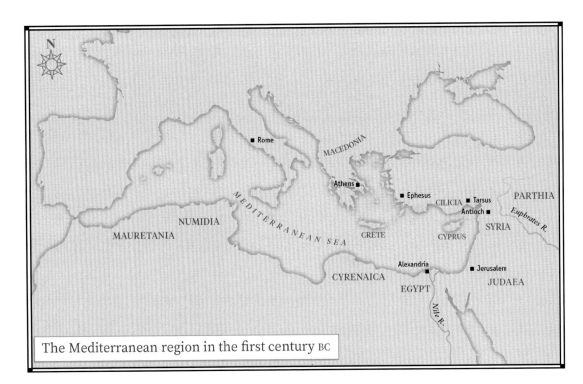

The Mediterranean region in the first century BC

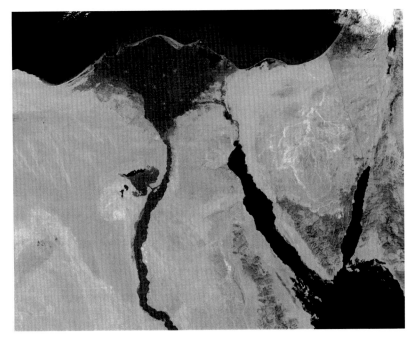

An aerial view of the Nile delta and part of the river. The dark portions show the vegetation in the fertile areas. The Egyptians called these areas kemet, or "black land," for the color of the soil. The deserts all around the Nile were known as deshret, or "red land." *Pexels*

brother, who ruled the island of Cyprus and could not afford to buy Rome's support. Possibly feeling justified by Ptolemy X's will, in 58 BC the Roman government took over Cyprus, leading Cleopatra's uncle to commit suicide.

The Alexandrians were outraged. Didn't Auletes care? Was he going to watch passively while Rome captured Cyprus? His unresponsiveness confirmed their opinion of the king as a weakling and a Roman pawn.

When Father's Away

Alexandrians' opposition became so intense that Auletes was eventually forced to flee in search of support. Initially he sought help from the Roman governor of Cyprus. The visit turned out to be unsuccessful and quite humiliating, because the governor had just taken a strong dose of laxatives and couldn't stand up to give the king a proper reception. Finally, Auletes continued to Rome, where he borrowed funds from moneylenders in order to buy the favor of influential men.

A Greek inscription suggests 11-year-old Cleopatra accompanied her father, but there is no other document confirming this. If this is true, the young girl would have had a first taste of preimperial Rome: a large but rather plain city with an intricate network of gloomy, narrow, and often unpaved alleys—quite different from the grandiose and cultured Alexandria, with its sunny, spacious seaport, enormous avenues, and impressive palaces.

Most likely, however, Cleopatra stayed in Alexandria, where the disgruntled citizens wasted no time in replacing her father with her sister Berenice, about seven years older than Cleopatra. This sudden, illegitimate takeover was Cleopatra's first personal experience of a lesson she had already learned from her family's history and would remember for the rest of her life: relatives can't be trusted.

Like her father, Berenice knew she needed Roman support, so she sent messengers to Rome to present her point of view: it looked as if Auletes had abandoned the throne, so the Roman government should recognize her as queen. In reality, her father had never resigned his position. As soon as he discovered her plot, he hired men to block the messengers by intimidating or bribing them. Some of the messengers (including their leader) were murdered. This caused a brief but widespread scandal, forcing Auletes to move again.

Finally, by offering a gift of 10,000 **talents**, the king was able to persuade the Roman governor of Syria, Aulus Gabinius, to help him regain his throne. In 55 BC Gabinius's army marched into Egypt and defeated the opposition, first in Pelusium, on the eastern edge of the Nile **delta**, and then in a brief battle on the way to Alexandria, where Berenice's husband, Archelaus (who was also her general), lost his life.

Auletes returned hastily home and had his daughter Berenice and her close followers executed. As for Archelaus, Auletes planned to let his body rot on the battlefield. But a young officer in Gabinius's army, Mark Antony (commonly known as Antony), persuaded him to give Archelaus a proper burial. According to Plutarch, Antony also prevented Auletes from massacring all those who had aligned themselves with Berenice—a merciful intervention that gained Antony the respect of Romans and Alexandrians alike.

Appian, a historian from Alexandria who wrote in the second century AD, said that Antony first saw the now 14-year-old Cleopatra at this time and fell in love with her. It is certainly possible, even if there aren't other documents to prove it.

Soon Gabinius and Antony left Egypt, leaving a large Roman army to protect Auletes. The king's victory must have been bittersweet. He was on the throne again but highly indebted to Rome and soured by his daughter's treason. In spite of this, he still nourished or at least wanted to convey hopes of harmony and peace among his remaining children, promoting them to the Egyptian people as "New Sibling-Loving Gods."

Auletes ruled Egypt four more years after his return to the throne. By this time, his wife, who had not been mentioned in official documents for a while, was most certainly dead, so he might have asked Cleopatra to assist him in some official duties, either to prepare her for the throne or simply to keep the male-female balance Egyptians greatly valued in their rulers. According to a few **Egyptologists**, inscriptions in the Temple of Hathor at Dendera that seem to link Auletes both to a Cleopatra and to an "eldest daughter of the king" support this theory.

In the final years of his life, Auletes wrote his last will, deposited one copy in the Library of Alexandria, and sent another one to Rome, expressly appointing the Roman people as protector and

Roman bust (head and shoulders) of Mark Antony. *Alinari / Art Resource, NY*

guardian of the new ruling couple. Who would they be?

A pharaoh was traditionally considered incomplete without a wife, but marrying someone from another family was dangerous and just not done in the Ptolemaic tradition. By arranging marriages between siblings or close relatives, they could prevent other families from gaining a right to the throne. When Auletes died in the spring of 51 BC, his decision was disclosed: 18-year-old Cleopatra and her 10-year-old brother Ptolemy XIII were to reign together.

11

BUILD AN EGYPTIAN-STYLE COLUMN

*Columns are some of the most interesting elements of Egyptian architecture. They were usually inspired by local plants. The columns' **shafts** were usually made to resemble tree trunks or bundles of reeds and were often decorated and painted. The **capitals** imitated typical Egyptian flowers or plants, such as the lotus, the lily, the papyrus flower (either closed or open), or the palm. In the Temple of Hathor in Dendera, the image of the goddess Hathor is carved on top of the columns.*

Make a column and carve its capital with an image that represents you or the area where you live—for example, a flower that is common in your region, a fruit you enjoy, your face, or your favorite possession. If you want to, you can also color it. Egyptian buildings and columns were once colorful, but the paint has faded with time. You can find some examples of colored columns here: https://traveltoeat.com /design-of-the-temple-of-isis-from-philae-egypt.

MATERIALS

- ½ pound air-drying modeling clay
- Plastic modeling tools
- Paintbrush and tempera or acrylic paints (optional)

1. Knead ½ pound modeling clay well, until it's soft. On a flat surface, roll the clay into a cylinder about 1 inch wide.

2. Gently pound one end of the cylinder down on your work surface to create a flat base that allows the column to stand.

2. With a modeling tool, make a mark about ¼ from the top of the cylinder. The shaft of your column will be below the mark, and the capital will be above it.

3. Decorate the shaft as you like. For example, you can make it look like a bundle of reeds by carving shallow, parallel vertical lines all around it and adding a set of two parallel horizontal

lines around the top and then the bottom of the shaft.

4. Now shape the capital in the image you have chosen. Don't worry about imperfections. They add to the antique look.

5. Dry your column by following the directions on the box.

6. Paint your column if you like.

7. When your column is finished, you can use it to hold up a small object.

The Fight for the Throne

The Queen, the Lady of the Two Lands, the goddess who loves her father. —Inscription on the Bucheion **stela** (commemorative stone)

Few Alexandrians mourned Ptolemy's death. Cleopatra showed him her allegiance by immediately adopting a second name: Philopator, "Father-loving." It was a fit indication of her desire to preserve many of her father's policies, especially in her alliance with Rome.

Sibling Rivalry

The ruling couple didn't fulfill their father's hopes as New Sibling-Loving Gods, however. In theory, Ptolemy XIII, as king, was the main power on the throne,

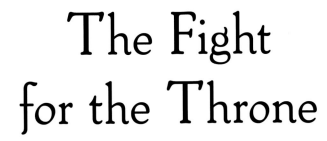

A typical representation of Cleopatra's first appearance in front of Caesar—a beautiful woman emerging from a Persian rug with perfectly tidy hair and clothes. *Duncan 1890, iStock*

and his advisers worked hard to make it so. In reality, at 18, Cleopatra was much more mature and, because of her experience with her father, better prepared to rule.

In the past, other Egyptian queens had been able to work well with less experienced kings, using their intelligence and diplomacy to strengthen the

This temple in Deir el-Bahri, near Luxor, was built in honor of the 18th Dynasty pharaoh Hatshepsut (known as "the female king"). After her death, people visited it to commemorate her life and offer sacrifices to her. *Werner Forman / Art Resource, NY*

union, but Cleopatra was very strong willed and, in this case, maybe shortsighted. It's possible that she tried to assume more power than her brother wanted to give her. Earlier documents include only Cleopatra's name, not her brother's, supporting this theory. In any case, she left Ptolemy under the control of his scheming advisers, who resented her and took every opportunity to turn the Alexandrians against her. After all, they could rule through the young Ptolemy but could never subdue the proud queen.

Raising an Army

By 49 BC Cleopatra seriously feared for her life. Together with some loyal followers, she sailed the Nile to the southern region of Thebes (today's Luxor), looking for support. Thebes was, at one time, the capital of Egypt and continued to be an important religious center, although it kept some feelings of superiority and resentment over the new "Greek" capital. Some historians believe the Thebans liked Cleopatra because, unlike other Ptolemies, she could speak their language. During the Ptolemies' rule, the region of Thebes was one of the most rebellious.

After this visit to Thebes, the young queen traveled northeast to Syria and Palestine, two states the Ptolemies had controlled for much of the third century BC. Travel in those days was lengthy, dangerous, and uncomfortable, but Cleopatra was determined. She needed to raise an army to stand up to her brother and either defeat him or regain her position of coruler.

A seasoned leader who had already gained a reputation and could inspire the trust of the troops might single-handedly raise an army, but women rarely accomplished this, especially not a dispossessed queen with feeble promises to offer. In spite of this, by the summer of 48, Cleopatra had gathered enough men and supplies to alarm her brother. This remarkable accomplishment is a testimony to her leadership skills, persuasion, and tenacity. Once again, her knowledge of languages must have also come in handy.

When Civil Wars Collide

While Cleopatra was away, Ptolemy XIII and his advisers hurried to erase her from all legal documents and persuaded (most likely with a bribe) the Roman government to recognize Ptolemy as sole ruler of Egypt, even if that meant voiding his father's will. It was an ideal situation Ptolemy wanted to maintain.

Ptolemy's army consisted of about 20,000 experienced soldiers, including both the Roman troops Gabinius had left behind and a mixed group of mercenaries. Heading the troops was Achillas, a bold and confident general. In terms of both size and skill, this army had the upper hand over Cleopatra's.

If Cleopatra's troops were inferior, they were still a threat, judging by the fact that the two armies remained locked for days in a cautious standoff at Pelusium.

It was during this tense confrontation that an unexpected visitor entered the scene: Pompey, a notable Roman general and politician who had just suffered a military defeat by his former friend, ally, and father-in-law, the Roman **consul** and general Julius Caesar. The conflict between these two men was part of a larger civil war, with Pompey representing a wide part of the Roman **Senate** who feared Caesar's growing power and independence as a threat to the **republic**.

Crushed but determined to gain the final victory, Pompey had sent messengers to Ptolemy XIII and set sail for Alexandria, where he expected a warm welcome and assistance from the young king, whose father Pompey had so often supported.

Head of Gnaeus Pompeius, also known as Pompey the Great.
Alinari / Art Resource

In the meantime, Ptolemy and his advisers had come to a different conclusion. Backing Pompey meant opposing Caesar, who appeared to be the likely winner in the war, and Egypt could survive only by siding with champions. When on September 28 Pompey's ships approached the Egyptian troops, Achillas led a greeting party out to sea, welcoming the Roman leader and inviting him to join him back to shore, where Ptolemy was waiting in his shining armor and purple robes.

Pompey agreed. It was only when he approached land that he realized it was a trap. Unable to defend himself, he covered his face with his **toga**, groaning as the Egyptians struck him repeatedly with swords and daggers. On his ships, everyone watched the murder with horror, including his wife, Cornelia, and 19-year-old son, Sextus, who had joined him on his travels to provide encouragement and comfort.

In the opposite camp, Cleopatra may have watched with equal surprise, but foul play was not alien to the Ptolemies, who seemed increasingly willing to resort to tricky or dishonorable actions to preserve their power.

When Caesar arrived in Alexandria on Pompey's heels a few days later, Ptolemy's tutor, Theodotus, hurried to give him the good news: his enemy was dead, thanks to the loyalty of the Egyptian king. As a token of allegiance, he presented Pompey's head and **signet ring**. Caesar's reaction was far from what the tutor had expected. Instead of showing delight, he turned away from Pompey's head in distress and wept over the ring. Honorable combat was one thing and deceitful behavior another. No respectable Roman would have wished such a gruesome death on his worst enemy.

Despite this upsetting sight, Caesar must also have felt relieved. The Roman civil war would soon be over. After giving orders for a proper **cremation** of Pompey's body and the delivery of the ashes to Cornelia, according to Roman customs, he marched his army along Canopic Way, a spacious avenue that led to the royal palace, where he had planned to set up his headquarters. In that dangerous environment where friends turned to enemies for convenience's sake, this march was a symbol of strength.

Ignoring the crowd's looks of deep resentment for what appeared to be a military takeover, he must have observed with interest the highly acclaimed cosmopolitan city. Caesar had an eye for detail. Besides, Alexandria was truly impressive. No matter how many scrolls had been written about its beauty, it never failed to astound visitors with its size, sophistication, and luxury. It was exotic and intriguing—an interesting hybrid of Greek culture and Egyptian traditions.

Caesar had several reasons to stay in Alexandria—including opposing winds at sea that would have made the trip to Rome too dangerous—and financial support was certainly a high priority.

After two years of civil war, he needed to raise money to pay his troops, and the Ptolemies were still financially indebted to Rome. First, however, he had to resolve the royals' disagreements.

To that end, he ordered Ptolemy XIII and Cleopatra to disband their armies and appear together to "settle their disputes by process of law before himself rather than by armed force between themselves." Ptolemy returned without recalling his troops, who maintained their blockade against his sister.

But Cleopatra was determined to plead her case to Caesar, and no military barrier could keep her away. No one knows how she managed to leave Pelusium undetected. Some historians believe she took a long detour first to the south and then to the west, in the company of a trusted Sicilian friend, Apollodorus. Once they reached the Nile, they could have sailed in a small boat to Alexandria, slipping quietly into the dock by the palace under cover of night.

Queen in a Blanket

The queen's appearance before Caesar is one of the most dramatic moments of her life story and has been told, retold, and embellished by authors, artists, and filmmakers. In Plutarch's original story, Apollodorus hid the queen "inside a bedsack" (most likely a linen sack used for carrying sheets), tied it "with a cord and carried it indoors to Caesar." This story gives us a possible clue as to her size—she must have been fairly small and light.

In any case, the story raises some questions. Would Caesar have allowed an unknown man with an uninspected sack into his private quarters? According to some sources, Cleopatra had sent messages to Caesar before her arrival, but would she have revealed such crucial information on paper, knowing how often dispatches were intercepted? If the news had fallen into the wrong hands, she could have lost her life. It's possible that Caesar knew she was coming but not the precise details. The sack might also have been opened outside Caesar's lodgings, allowing her to fix her hair and clothes after a long trip through hot and sandy deserts and on the misty Nile. One way or another, the scene was probably different from what is portrayed in movies and artwork.

Cleopatra may have looked different from what modern representations suggest. For example, some coins issued during her rule show her with a hooked nose and a pointed chin, both features that were common to the Ptolemies. Then again, in an era without television, newspapers, or the internet, images of rulers were not meant to correspond to reality. In this case, the coins' message was simple: Cleopatra was a true member of the Ptolemaic dynasty and ought to be respected as such.

Because art was used as **propaganda**—meant to sway public opinion—there is no reliable image of Cleopatra. Roman **busts** show a classic female ruler of the **Hellenistic** period, wearing the

Cleopatra portrayed on a silver coin. *Classical Numismatic Group, www.cngcoins.com*

distinctive Greek headband, while Egyptian art displays a typical queen who could hardly be distinguished from the others.

Whatever her appearance, 21-year-old Cleopatra was charming and interesting. According to Plutarch, her beauty "was in itself not altogether incomparable, nor such as to strike those who saw her." He agreed that she was attractive, but for other reasons: in conversations she "had an irresistible charm," and her presence, the persuasiveness of her words, and her way of dealing with others "had something stimulating about it."

As for Caesar, in spite of his age, 52, and fast-receding hairline (which caused him great embarrassment), he was still considered quite handsome and had a reputation for being a ladies' man. Like Cleopatra, he had a magnetic personality. In fact, the two leaders had many things in common. They were both intelligent, literate, witty, charismatic, ambitious, and ready to do anything to achieve their goals. They were both fiercely hated by some people and deeply loved by others. They were people of action and had taken great risks in their lives. Finally, they were both interested—for

MAKE EGYPTIAN BREATH FRESHENERS

Although the Egyptians had many advanced medical practices for the time, dental health was something they had not yet mastered. What's more, the stones they used to grind flour left grit and sand in their bread, which wore down tooth enamel. Archaeologists have found poor and infected teeth in several **mummies**, *even those of young people. Poor teeth and gum health can lead to bad breath. To remedy the situation, people created what might have been the first breath fresheners in history, "a combination of* **frankincense**, **myrrh** *and cinnamon boiled with honey and shaped into pellets," and Cleopatra might very well have used them—maybe even before her encounter with Caesar. Try something similar and see how it might have tasted.*

ADULT SUPERVISION REQUIRED

Yields about 6 penny-size pellets

MATERIALS

- 1 tablespoon pure raw honey (solid)
- 1 quart-sized microwave-safe bowl
- Microwave oven
- 1 teaspoon cinnamon
- Oven mitts
- Olive oil
- Spoon
- Small plate

1. Place 1 tablespoon of raw honey in a microwave-safe bowl and micro-wave for 10 seconds.

2. Add 1 teaspoon of cinnamon and stir well.

3. Microwave the mix-ture for 1 minute. Watch to make sure it doesn't overflow.

4. Using oven mitts to lift the hot bowl, carefully place it in the fridge. Let it cool for 5–10 minutes or until the mixture is cool and stringy.

5. Place a few drops of olive oil in your palm and rub your hands together. This will prevent the honey from sticking to your hands.

6. Spoon out about ¼ teaspoon of the mixture and roll it between your fingers or palms until you make a round pellet.

7. Rub a little oil on a small plate and place the pellet on the plate. Repeat step 5 for the rest of the mixture. You should end up with about 6 pellets.

8. Enjoy immediately or place in the fridge to harden even more. Once the pellets are hardened, they can be stored at room temperature.

different reasons—in keeping Egypt prosperous and strong.

Cleopatra's position on the throne—in fact, her very life—was at stake. Given her brother's military and political power, an alliance with Caesar was her best chance of survival, at least in her country. For Caesar, a strong and stable Egypt meant a steady supply of support for his troops and a way to strengthen his reputation by consolidating an important and fruitful alliance for his country.

The Alexandrian War

Whatever happened that night, the next morning Ptolemy XIII woke up to terrible news: his sister was in the palace, had already talked to Caesar, and had convinced him to support her cause. Feeling deceived, Ptolemy left the palace screaming accusations of betrayal, tossed away his crown, and fell to the ground in tears. The crowd, traditionally opposed to Rome and disposed to rioting, joined his protest by pressing toward the palace doors.

Keeping his poise, Caesar appeared briefly in their presence, assuring them he only wanted to carry out Auletes's will. He again called for a formal meeting between Ptolemy XIII and Cleopatra, requesting they work together. To appease all parties, he returned the island of Cyprus to Egypt, under the joint rule of Cleopatra's youngest siblings, her 11-year-old brother Ptolemy XIV and sister Arsinoe IV, who was just a few years younger than Cleopatra.

For most people, it was not a satisfying solution. The Alexandrians didn't want closer Roman oversight, and Ptolemy XIII didn't want equal standing with his sister. Instead of complying, he summoned his army and arranged his warships in the harbor, while the Alexandrians continued to attack Caesar's troops in an informal, guerrilla-war fashion.

Fighting in Alexandria was a new challenge for Caesar, who was not used to battle within the confines of a city, with enemies hiding in every corner, ready to attack day and night. Besides being more numerous, the Alexandrians were armed with the type of heroic fury that comes from desperation. If Caesar was not expelled, they were convinced that Egypt would become another Roman province.

Caesar had already sent for reinforcements from his troops in neighboring countries, but he knew full well it would take weeks before their arrival. In the meantime, he seized Ptolemy and locked him in the palace to prevent him from doing more damage.

Apparently Cleopatra didn't participate in the war, instead following the news in the protection of the guarded palace. Surely she was alarmed when she heard that Caesar almost lost his life in a naval battle and had to swim to shore, holding his important documents out of the water with one hand. He was her only hope of survival. His defeat would mean her death.

While Cleopatra awaited the war's outcome, Arsinoe escaped from the palace and, supported by her influential tutor Ganymede, persuaded the Alexandrian people to crown her queen. From the palace, Pothinus, Ptolemy XIII's main adviser, followed the events with hope. He planned to find a way to leave the palace with Ptolemy and join the angry rebels outside. He revealed this plot in a note to Achillas, encouraging him to work with Arsinoe for the time being, in spite of disagreements. The message, however, was intercepted, and Caesar had Pothinus killed.

Without Pothinus's help, the disagreements among Caesar's leading enemies worsened. Finally, a quarrel between Achillas and Ganymede motivated Arsinoe to have Achillas murdered and to put Ganymede in his place as commander. Within a short period, Ptolemy lost both his top general and his chief adviser.

Ganymede proved to be a clever leader. Even Caesar had to admit it when the tutor found a way to pollute the palace's water by diverting saltwater into its pipes. It was an ingenious move. Caesar's soldiers could live without food for some time but not without water. They begged Caesar to return to Rome. Caesar explained it was too late. The Alexandrians would most likely kill them as they tried to leave.

Besides, all was not lost. While the Egyptians got their water from the Nile, people in most parts of the world used wells. Well water was probably safer to drink, too, because the Nile was also used for bathing, for washing clothes and utensils, and as a sewer. In the end, after many hours of hard digging, Caesar's men struck groundwater and quenched their thirst.

Through all this, Ptolemy remained in the palace with Cleopatra and Caesar. But eventually,

frustrated with Ganymede's heavy-handed rule, the Alexandrians asked Caesar to release Ptolemy. They promised they would stop the fighting if Ptolemy was released.

Ptolemy tearfully pleaded with Caesar not to make him leave the palace. In reality, he was trying to trick the Roman general into doing just that. Caesar could easily see through the deception. Weighing the situation, however, he determined that the inexperienced king couldn't do much harm outside the palace. Besides, if the teenager turned against him, the Roman general would have reason to deny him the throne.

As expected, as soon as he left the palace, Ptolemy assumed command of his troops in a fiercer assault. At that point, however, Caesar's allies were approaching with a large army.

At dawn on March 27, by the Nile delta, Caesar and his forces attacked Ptolemy's army, destroying it. Ptolemy tried to escape by boarding an overcrowded boat. But the boat overturned, and the heavily armored king drowned.

That night, Caesar raced victorious into Alexandria with his cavalry. Cleopatra must have breathed a sigh of relief. After years of turmoil and insecurity, there was hope for her reign and future.

A large crowd of Alexandrians rushed to meet Caesar at the gates and beg him for mercy. He could have easily killed them, but it would have been useless bloodshed. So he spared them. What's more, he did not make Egypt an official Roman province and end the country's independence, as the Alexandrians had so feared. At that

MAKE A JACK-O'-LANTERN LIGHTHOUSE

From his window in the palace, Caesar could see one of the seven wonders of the ancient world: a huge, three-level lighthouse on the island of Pharos, just off the coast of Alexandria and connected to the city by a long strip of land. It was over 300 feet tall (taller than a 30-story skyscraper) and made of white stone. He called it "a work of wonderful construction."

The top story of the Alexandrian lighthouse included one or two huge mirrors made of polished metal, which reflected the sun's rays by day and the glow of a large fire by night. It was so bright that the light could be seen 30 miles out.

To learn how mirrors can change a beam of light, you can make a small imitation lighthouse using a butternut squash. If you do it at the end of October, you can use it as a Halloween decoration!

ADULT SUPERVISION REQUIRED

MATERIALS

- Pumpkin-carving or other sharp knife
- Ripe butternut squash
- Spoon
- Apple corer
- Marker
- 3-inch frameless mirror
- Flameless tea-light candle
- Camera (optional)

1. Ask an adult to help you cut off the top and bottom of a ripe butternut squash. Set the top aside to use later.

2. Use a spoon to scoop out the seeds from the bottom and an apple corer to scoop out the pulp from the top.

3. With a marker, draw a design on one side of the squash, what will now be the front of your lantern. You can draw simple rectangular doors on the top and bottom (to copy the Alexandrian lighthouse), a jack-o'-lantern face, or whatever you wish.

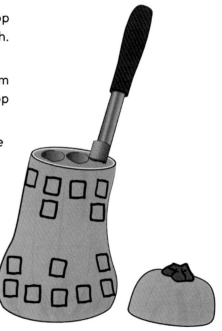

4. With an adult's help, carefully cut out the designs you drew.

5. With an adult's help, starting from the bottom of the squash, cut a straight slit on each side, about 1–1½ inch from the back (close to the back but without cutting off a piece of the squash). The slit should be as long as your mirror.

6. Slide the mirror into the slit you created so that the reflective side is facing the front of the squash.

7. In a room that gets dark, turn on a flameless tea-light candle and place it on a flat surface. Then place the squash over the candle, making sure the candle is in front of the mirror.

8. Put the top back on the squash, and turn off the lights.

9. How does your lantern look? Experiment by taking out the mirror. Do you see a difference? Does the mirror make the light shine brighter? In a different direction? By taking a picture in the dark, you can capture the direction of the light rays.

You can try other combinations. For example, you could make the incisions closer to the front of the squash, and insert two mirrors joining at an angle. Notice the difference.

PREPARE HOMEMADE YOGURT

The Egyptians might have built up a resistance to the bacteria and other impurities in the Nile's water, but it was not very healthy. Most of the time they drank beer and milk. The beer was made from barley and was probably less alcoholic than it is now. Even children could drink it. To make the most of milk, which soured quickly, the Egyptians made a fermented drink that was similar to yogurt.

Try making yogurt at home. Start with a small batch until you better understand the process. You can make larger quantities once you become a pro.

ADULT SUPERVISION REQUIRED

MATERIALS

- 1 cup whole milk
- Small saucepan
- Stove
- Food thermometer
- Small glass container with lid
- 1 tablespoon plain yogurt with live active cultures
- Spoon
- Terry hand towel
- Insulated lunch box
- Colander (optional)
- Cheesecloth (optional)

1. With an adult's help, bring 1 cup of whole milk to a boil in a small saucepan on the stove.

2. Once it reaches a boil, remove the saucepan from the heat. Using the food thermometer, check periodically until the milk is about 100–115 degrees Fahrenheit.

3. Pour the milk into a small glass container with a lid.

4. Add 1 tablespoon of plain yogurt and stir gently.

5. Put the lid on the glass container, making sure it's firmly sealed; then wrap the container in a terry hand towel, and place it in an insulated lunch box.

6. After 5–6 hours, gently remove the container from the lunch box and towel. You can see if the milk is firm by turning the container slightly without having to open it. If it's not, wrap it again, return it to the lunch box, and leave it 3–5 more hours (it might take up to 10 hours to turn into yogurt; try not to disturb it too often).

7. Once the milk is the thickness of typical yogurt, it's ready! For a thicker yogurt, you may strain it through a colander lined with cheesecloth. Be sure to refrigerate your yogurt until you are ready to eat it. It will keep in the refrigerator for about two weeks.

Home-made yogurt is delicious. You may have to experiment a few times to get it just right. Once you are satisfied with your results, you may use 1 tablespoon of your home-made yogurt to make a new batch.

Obviously Egyptians didn't have insulated lunch boxes or thermometers. They tested the temperature by hand (it should be as warm as comfortable bath water) and let the milk ferment in the sun's heat. You can do the same if you live in a hot climate (wrap the container in a towel first). With an adult's help, you can also place the wrapped container in your oven if it has a pilot light. In that case, preheat the oven to 170 degrees Fahrenheit, turn it off, and place the wrapped container inside (make sure it doesn't directly touch any hot surface as too much heat kills the bacteria).

unstable time of civil wars, any Roman put in charge of such a bountiful and large area could take advantage of his wealth and power to rise to a higher position in the Roman government and demand more authority than he was allowed to have. Instead, Caesar chose to place Cleopatra back on her throne, together with her only surviving brother, 12-year-old Ptolemy XIV, in an arrangement similar to the one she had with Ptolemy XIII. He also kept Cyprus under Egyptian rule but stripped Arsinoe of all her power; she was captured as a traitor and sent to Rome in chains.

Finally, Caesar decreed that three (later four) Roman military units of about 5,000 men each, called **legions**, would support the new Egyptian rulers as long as the couple remained faithful to Rome. "If they proved ungrateful," he wrote, "those same troops could hold them in check." The Ptolemies' longstanding dependence on Rome had reached its peak. The proud kingdom of Egypt had fully become a client state, formally self-ruling but still subject to Rome's power.

Cleopatra's Cruise

[Egypt] has the most wonders, and everywhere presents works beyond description. —Herodotus

With the exhausting Alexandrian War behind him, Caesar was free to return to Rome. He had been in Egypt for nine months and away from his country for over a year. He had much pressing business to settle and more victories to gain against enemies who had taken advantage of his absence. Besides, winter was over and spring would be a safer time for navigation and war. Instead of going home, however, according to early historians, he decided to stay in Egypt a little longer—maybe as long as three months—to take a trip with Cleopatra on the Nile.

Pyramids at Giza. *Wikimedia Commons/AWIB-ISAW*

Up the River

A leisure cruise seems like an odd choice at a time of civil war, especially for a top military officer who had been extraordinarily active and focused. Was he physically exhausted? Depressed? He had for some time been strangely lax in his communications with Rome, cutting off all his correspondence after his arrival in Egypt. Initially he was justified. Sending messengers in the heat of battle was not easy. Yet he kept quiet even after the war. Some Romans were quick to blame the mysterious Cleopatra, who they said had bewitched and immobilized the valiant Roman general.

According to Appian, Caesar went "exploring the country." Being naturally curious about the world around him, he wanted to learn about the source of the Nile, which was still unknown at that time. In fact, his contemporary poet Lucan explained Caesar had discussed this subject with one of Cleopatra's priests.

In any case, it was common for pharaohs like Cleopatra to take their important guests on a tour of the land, or at least of the closest tourist attractions, either in Alexandria (site of the renowned tomb of Alexander the Great) or in the nearby Memphis region (just south of today's Cairo), with its astounding Pyramids of Giza, a curious labyrinth (an actual maze or a large temple with a complicated floor plan), and the popular city of Crocodilopolis (where visitors could feed the sacred crocodile).

(left) **Front of an Egyptian chest, showing a king making an offering to the crocodile-god Sobek. The chest might have been used in temple rituals.** *The Walters Art Museum, Baltimore*

(right) **A modern-day Nile valley farmer. Many Egyptians still live much like they did in ancient times.** *Dale Haussner, Flickr*

Quite likely, Caesar was also hoping to explore some of Egypt's abundant resources, and a trip on the Nile allowed him to observe firsthand the long and narrow valley that yielded most of the area's agricultural products: rich fields of wheat and barley, varied orchards, vineyards, fruitful palm trees, and long lines of papyrus reeds, which were used to create the most valuable type of paper at that time.

The main reason for the trip, however, might have been political, since a large number of Caesar's troops, traveling in a separate 400-ship fleet, escorted their boat. Since most of the Egyptian population resided in the Nile valley, this official trip would have made a much-needed statement after years of political uncertainty: the queen is the legitimate ruler under the protection of Rome. This would have contributed to national security, to the benefit of both Cleopatra and Caesar.

It was not a new practice. Without the advantage of modern mass media, the pharaohs often traveled up and down the Nile, together with court officials, soldiers, and scribes, to reassure (or, in some cases, warn) the people of their continued presence and rule. What's more, since Egyptians believed that their gods moved along the Nile, the pharaohs' trips reminded the people of the divine nature of their rulers.

Exploring Egypt's Riches

Cleopatra was certainly familiar with the history of pharaohs, which was already documented and organized, as it still is, into 30 dynasties. Both she and Caesar were also acquainted with the writings of Herodotus, a famous fifth-century BC Greek historian who had inspired hundreds of contemporary and future travelers with his descriptions of

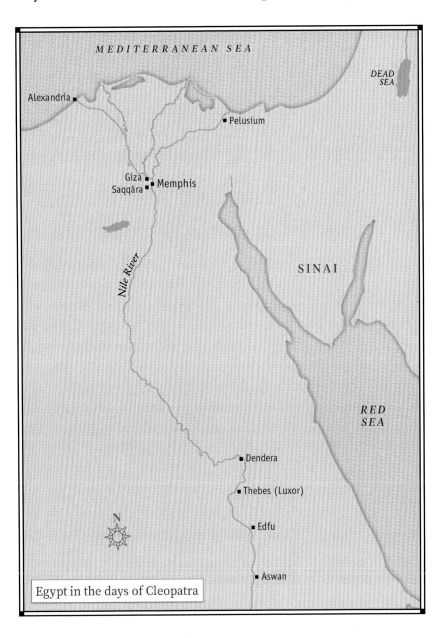

Egypt in the days of Cleopatra

The Nile River. *Ron Kline, Flickr*

to accept new seed, the ground yielded mud for bricks, and the shore was filled with stranded fish that could be eaten or salted for later use.

That the Nile runs toward the north was another bonus because the prevailing wind blew north to south. A boat could then follow the stream when traveling north (or use oars if the travelers were in a hurry) and raise its sails to be carried south by the wind. Because of this ease of travel, the Nile was Egypt's main route. Unlike the Romans, the Egyptians never bothered to build an efficient network of roads across their country's inhospitable desert terrain.

The Nile, however, was not the only source of amazement for visitors of Egypt. To Herodotus, the country possessed "the most wonders" and "works beyond description." Caesar didn't have to go far to realize the truth of that appraisal. About 150 miles southeast of Alexandria, just before the Nile breaks into its delta, he would have seen the astonishing pyramids complex at Giza, a desert cemetery built for Fourth Dynasty kings about 2,500 years earlier. Even for Caesar and Cleopatra, those were ancient works—more ancient than Cleopatra is to us today.

The main buildings—the Great Pyramid of Khufu, the Pyramid of Khafre (Khufu's son), and the Pyramid of Menkaure (Khafre's son)—were clearly visible from the river, surprising visitors with their enormous size (481, 448, and 203 feet tall, respectively) that was yet impeccably proportionate to the apparent immensity of the desert surrounding them. No human-made building had ever reached those heights. The first two

Egypt. In fact, Caesar might have shared Herodotus's feelings of awe and bewilderment as he explored his surroundings, starting with the first natural source of Egypt's wealth—the Nile. "The Egyptians have a climate peculiar to themselves," the Greek traveler wrote, "and their river is different in its nature from all other rivers."

To a European, the Nile was definitely unusual. Unlike most rivers, it ran from south to north and rose dramatically between July and October, when most rivers are low due to the heat. To Egyptians, the Nile's yearly rising was a sign of the gods' favor, because the flooding waters brought an abundance of benefits. When the mineral-rich waters retreated slowly after a flood, the fields were ready

The three main pyramids of Giza. *Juan David Martinez, Flickr*

pyramids, still mostly covered in the original white limestone (today visible only on top of the Pyramid of Khafre), especially looked like perfectly symmetrical glowing mountains pointing to the sky.

To see these monuments up close, Caesar and Cleopatra would have had to leave the boat and be transported on hand-carried carriages, called **litters**, over a sandy path built for that purpose, across the dry, sterile land that allowed for nearly perfect preservation of both mummies and treasures. Up close, the pyramids' size would have seemed even more imposing.

Next to the pyramids, they would have seen the Great **Sphinx**, also built by Khafre—an enormous statue with a pharaoh's head and a lion's body, crouching as a wary guardian of the sacred grounds, looking steadily into the horizon or, in the words of the American author Mark Twain, "gazing out over the ocean of Time."

The Great Sphinx. *Fèlix Vila, Flickr*

HOW THE PYRAMIDS WERE BUILT

Initially most people in Egypt were buried in pits underground, but this method didn't provide a safe place for the bodies. Kings, who were expected to live forever in the afterlife, especially needed a spacious room with storage facilities, and their architects developed what is now called a *mastaba*, a low, rectangular mud-brick or stone building with one or more underground burial chambers.

In the 27th century BC, an architect named Imhotep decided to top the *mastaba* with another *mastaba*, to be used as a visiting room for those who wanted to pay respect to the dead. He then kept piling *mastabas* one on top of another until he arrived at the six-stepped pyramid of Saqqâra, the oldest pyramid existing today.

Later architects tried to create a smooth-sided pyramid. After a few failed attempts, they mastered a technique that was used in what is known as the Red Pyramid because of its red bricks. Originally, this pyramid was entirely covered with white limestone, which was removed and reused for buildings in Cairo during the Middle Ages.

The limestone was brought by boat from a quarry across the Nile, while the stone used for the pyramids' interiors was normally taken from nearby quarries. Pink granite, mostly used in burial chambers, came from Elephantine (modern Aswan), at the southern edge of the country. The stones were probably brought to the building site by heavy wooden sleds pulled along specially prepared roads or over rollers laid on the ground.

According to Herodotus, it took 100,000 men 20 years to finish the Great Pyramid, working in shifts of three months per year. Since most of the Egyptians were farmers who could work the land only after the Nile's yearly flooding, it's possible that pharaohs hired these men during their off months (about three months out of the year) and that 100,000 was a rounded estimation of all the men employed in the course of 20 years. The notion that the pyramids were built by slaves is a rather modern idea that is not confirmed by historical records.

The Step Pyramid of Saqqâra. *Prof. Richard Mortel, Riyadh*

Sharing in the Glory

If Caesar had been impressed by the Alexandrian lighthouse, he would have found the pyramids even more stunning. As a leader, he must have realized the organizational skills necessary to build these imposing monuments in a relatively short time (before the death of their intended occupants). Egypt's architectural achievements, along with the fact that the country had stayed unified for over 3,000 years, might have encouraged some thoughts he had been entertaining for a while on the importance of a strong ruler.

At that time, the Roman republican system, which had lasted since 509 BC with a limited centralized power, seemed inadequate to face the challenges of Rome's extended territories, including a greater need for defense and supplies. The office of **dictator**, created as a short-term emergency measure (it was intended to last six months at the most), was becoming almost indispensable on a long-term basis. Could Rome ever attain the order and stability that seemed necessary to achieve great things and last thousands of years?

On the royal barge, Caesar and Cleopatra had plenty of time to talk about these things. He would have learned about the 42 districts of Egypt, each overseen by a governor. In fact, he probably met some of those governors along the way, as they normally prepared the special palaces built for regal visits (known as "the **mooring places** of the pharaohs") and for replenishing the royal boats with fresh bread, meat, fruits, and vegetables. These stops would have given Cleopatra opportunities to confer with the governors, who had a chance to display loyalty to the crown, and meet with the priests, who would once again show gratitude and recognition of her generosity to their temples.

Caesar would have realized the exceptional influence pharaohs had on their people and their importance as reassuring symbols of the Egyptian concept of *maat* (a combination of justice, truth, and order, which is the opposite of *ifset*, chaos). Pharaohs were practically the owners of Egypt, in possession of all its land, wealth, and inhabitants. In fact, even though the Egyptian religion taught that there was a difference between gods and rulers, people ended up worshiping their pharaohs as gods—more specifically as earthly incarnations of the Egyptian god Horus, son of Osiris and Isis.

Caesar would have seen Cleopatra fit naturally into that role, often donning her official attire, executing orders with confidence, and receiving with grace the praises of the people who ran to shore to see the barge pass by. Standing next to her, he shared in the glory as her divine escort.

Farther South

No one knows how far south Cleopatra took Caesar down the 750-mile-long Nile valley, but probably not farther than the ancient city of Thebes, which had been the capital of Egypt for almost 1,000 years. Thebes had its own burial grounds, now known as the Valley of the Kings and Valley of the Queens. This group of tombs was built from the 18th to the 20th Dynasty inside natural rock

MUMMIFY A HOT DOG

Ancient Egyptians believed the human life force (called ka) could only survive in a well-preserved body after death. Noticing that bodies buried in the hot desert sand preserved better than under other types of soil (the dryness stopped bacteria reproduction), Egyptian priests perfected a complicated drying system, removing the internal organs, which were dried with a chemical called natron and then preserved in special containers (called canopic jars). Only the heart remained in the body. The brain, which was considered useless, was thrown away.

The body was also dried with natron and then tightly wrapped with pieces of linen or reused papyrus covered with plaster. After many layers, this casing (called cartonnage) was painted, then placed in a coffin (also called a sarcophagus). This process is called **mummification**.

To get the hang of mummification, try mummifying a hot dog. Instead of natron, you will use a mixture of salt and baking soda for drying your "mummy."

MATERIALS

- 4 cups salt
- 2 cups baking soda
- Mixing bowl
- Fork
- Rectangular container, a little larger than the hot dog, with lid
- Hot dog
- 10 squares toilet paper, still connected
- Roll of gauze
- Small bowl
- 3 tablespoons plaster of paris
- 1½ tablespoons water
- Hair dryer
- Markers

1. Place 2 cups of salt and 1 cup of baking soda in a mixing bowl and mix well with a fork.

2. Pour some of this mixture in the bottom of a rectangular container until it coats the bottom and is about ½ inch high. Place the hot dog on top of the mixture.

3. Completely cover the hot dog with the rest of the mixture and put the lid on the container. Leave the hot dog in the container with the lid closed at room temperature for seven days.

4. After a week, remove the hot dog. It should be much smaller and almost completely dry.

5. Repeat steps 1–4 with the same hot dog but with a new salt and baking soda mixture.

6. This time, leave the closed container at room temperature for 10 days before removing the hot dog. The salt and baking soda mixture should be completely dry, showing that the drying process is complete.

7. Wrap the dry hot dog with a length of about 10 squares of toilet paper.

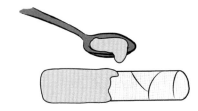

8. Wrap gauze around the hot dog, first lengthwise, then all around it, leaving no exposed areas.

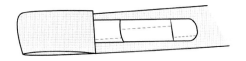

9. In a small bowl, mix 3 tablespoons of plaster of paris with a little water. Start with a few drops and increase slowly until you reach the consistency of Greek yogurt, up to 1½ tablespoons.

10. Place the wrapped hot dog in the empty open container, then spoon a thin layer of plaster over it, just enough to cover all the gauze and keep it sealed.

11. Dry immediately with a hot hair dryer to prevent moisture from seeping into the hot dog.

12. Use markers to decorate your mummy.

You may get some ideas from the image on this page.

For variety, you can mummify a zucchini or a carrot. For the zucchini, you should take out the core with an apple corer and fill it with the salt and baking soda mixture. In both cases, you will need to replace the mixture twice, leaving the vegetables in the mixture for a total of 20 days for the carrot and 40 days for the zucchini.

A mummy case of an unknown woman.
The Walters Art Museum, Baltimore

MAKE A SIMPLE RIVER BOAT

By the time Cleopatra was queen, Egypt had all kinds of ships and boats that were similar to those used by other powerful Mediterranean countries. Cleopatra's royal barge might have resembled that of her ancestor Ptolemy IV—an enormous and luxurious cruiser about 300 feet long (approximately as long as an American football field), 45 feet wide, and 60 feet tall, with lavishly decorated bedrooms and halls. Farmers and fishermen, by contrast, still used simple reed boats, just as their forefathers had done for thousands of years.

You can make a model of a simple river boat using straws instead of reeds.

MATERIALS

- 25–30 plastic flexible drinking straws
- Duct tape

1. Insert the bottom of one straw into the bottom of another straw by squeezing the bottom end of the first straw. Bend the flexible tops on each side to create an angle.

2. Do the same with three more pairs of straws. You should have four pairs.

3. Lay two of these pairs on a flat surface so that they meet at both ends. The straws should together create a long hexagon. These will be the outer edges of your boat.

4. From a new straw, cut two 1½-inch pieces (not the flexible part), and place the pieces perpendicularly inside the hexagon, about 3 inches apart and with the ends touching the sides of the hexagon.

5. Using duct tape, tape the two small pieces to the sides of the hexagon, then tape the two ends of the hexagon together.

6. Take one of the remaining pairs of straws and tape each end to the ends of the hexagon, alongside one of the first pairs. Do this with the other remaining pair, taping it to the ends alongside the other outer-edge pair. These two new pairs should be toward what will be the center of your boat. This will be the frame of your boat.

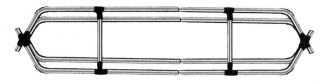

7. Fill in the rest of the boat around the frame by taking 10 more straws all going the same direction, bunching them

together, and taping the bundle at the flexible top end to one end of the boat. Squeeze tightly.

8. Cut a 6-inch piece of duct tape. Then cut it in half lengthwise to make two thinner strips.

9. Wrap one strip around the new straws just below the flexible bend and the other close to the bottom ends, bundling the new straws.

10. Cut about 2½ inches off the bottom end of 10 more straws, then join them to the 10 you just added by squeezing the bottom end of one and inserting it into the end of another.

11. With the unused thin strip of tape (from step 9), join the tops of these new straws together to the other end of the boat. Squeeze tightly.

12. Add additional straws or portions of straws where you see any holes, always taping them to the frame. Your boat is ready to float!

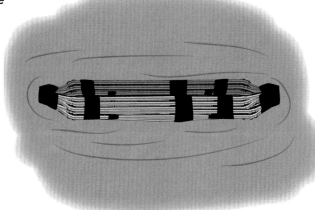

EGYPTIAN ART

For Egyptians, art was not about creativity. It was meant to portray ideas and followed very strict rules. For example, a temple image of a pharaoh crushing his enemies inspired confidence in his strength, while a tomb painting of a fruitful field promised abundance in the afterlife.

Egyptian portraits didn't necessarily look like the people they represented. Most of their rulers had a standard look. Queens were always slim, and kings were always strong. Social status was marked by the type of clothing and by the perspective. Important characters were depicted as larger than the others.

In addition, the preservation of the current order was entrenched in the Egyptian mentality. They were cautious about implementing innovations, especially those that seemed unnecessary and potentially dangerous. Because of this, only experts can notice small differences in Egyptian art in the course of 3,000 years. To the untrained eye, the style appears amazingly consistent over time. (By contrast, think how much European or American art has changed just within a few centuries, and how many different styles there are now.)

The only exception to this constant Egyptian style happened during the rule of 18th Dynasty pharaoh Akhenaten, who completely disrupted his country's traditions by proclaiming the existence of only one god (the sun-god Aten) and allowing artists to draw and paint what they wanted. In fact, he seems to have encouraged lifelike everyday scenes. For example, one relief sculpture shows Akhenaten and his wife enjoying their children as common parents do, instead of the usual images of pharaohs fighting or offering sacrifices to the gods. After Akhenaten's death, art and religion returned quickly to their traditional ways.

A painting in the tomb of Nebamun, 18th Dynasty. Nebamun is standing on a reed boat in papyrus marshes while throwing a hunting stick to catch birds. Nebamun's wife and daughter (who wears the "side-lock" hairstyle typical of children) look on. *Erich Lessing / Art Resource, NY*

cliffs, after the treasure-filled pyramids had been repeatedly robbed.

By the time Cleopatra became a ruler, however, many of these new tombs had also been looted and their walls blackened by campfires or filled with tourists' graffiti. Since the raided tombs were already opened, she might have taken her important visitor inside. Caesar, who was used to the Roman custom of cremating the dead (an abomination to the Egyptians), must have been generally intrigued by Egypt's rituals and practices. No one knows what he or Cleopatra believed regarding the afterlife. Both had been instructed in Greek philosophy, which regarded the body as a prison of the soul and virtually useless after death. In any case, as pharaoh, Cleopatra actively promoted her country's religious practices, participating in all the big functions and supporting the priests with both money and supplies.

According to the Roman historian Suetonius, Caesar would have liked to continue sailing almost as far as Ethiopia (a general name used to indicate the lands south of Egypt)—a desire Cleopatra most likely shared, if for no other reason than to keep spreading her message of political stability all the way to the southern borders—but "his soldiers refused to follow him." The cause of this refusal is unknown. Maybe they feared that Caesar's prolonged absence from the lingering civil war could be damaging to Rome. In any case, Caesar knew it was time to return to face both his enemies and his duties.

DRAW AND COLOR LIKE AN ANCIENT EGYPTIAN

Egyptians often decorated their tombs with favorite scenes of life on earth or joyful scenes they expected to find in the afterlife. You may choose to draw a scene of your daily life or something you love to do.

MATERIALS

- 8½-by-11-inch ½-inch-grid paper
- Pencil
- Colored pencils, crayons, markers, or watercolors

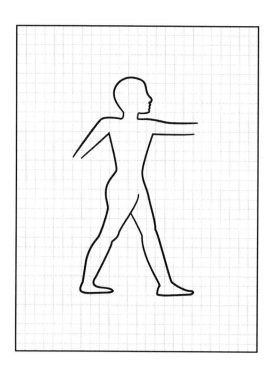

1. Egyptian artists used a grid to get the proportions of the human body right. Generally, you should plan about five squares from the shoulders to the waist, five squares from the waist to the knees, and five squares from the knees to the ankles.

2. Draw your figure following the same rules Egyptians used for thousands of years: head, arms, legs, hips, and feet turned sideways, and shoulders and chest facing the viewer.

3. Draw an eye on the face, as if it were facing the viewer. Add a curved eyebrow.

4. Draw a black wig, leaving the ear showing. Men's wigs usually looked like a helmet. Women's wigs were long and straight.

5. Add a short skirt for a man or a long, tight dress for a woman (she will look as if she is wearing leggings). You can also add jewelry and draw an object in his or her hand.

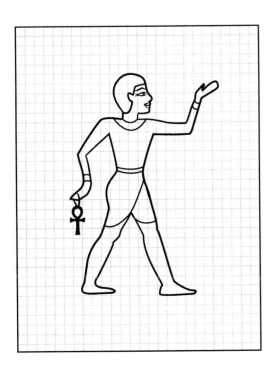

6. If you want to, you may draw a smaller figure next to this. If you do, it will show someone less important, not necessarily smaller or younger. Remember to keep the proportions equal. For example, this time do three squares for each measurement instead of five.

7. Color your figures using bright colors. In Egyptian paintings, women had yellow skin and men reddish-brown skin, no matter what their true colors were (probably because men spent more time in the sun). The background was left blank. You can look at the painting on the cover of this book for an example of vivid Egyptian colors.

The New Goddess Isis

The female Horus, the great one, mistress of perfection, brilliant in counsel, Mistress of the Two Lands, Cleopatra, the goddess who loves her father. —Inscription on the Armant birth house

I hate the queen. —Cicero

Caesar moved quickly to counteract the blows his enemies had dealt his armies in his absence. He immediately defeated King Pharnaces II of Bosporus (a region in today's Turkey) in a battle so swift that he summarized it "Veni, Vidi, Vici" (I came, I saw, I conquered). A longer battle against a coalition of his enemy Pompey's supporters, backed by King Juba I of Numidia (a small state on the North African coast), almost ended in defeat. Ultimately,

The motif of Cleopatra-Isis and her son Caesarion is found again in the huge relief sculpture on the rear wall of the Temple of Hathor at Dendera (Hathor was very similar to Isis). *Manna Nader, Gabana Studios, Cairo*

in spite of the unfamiliar desert environment and the swift surprise tactics of the Numidians, Caesar succeeded. The war ended with the death of his foremost opponents, who chose suicide over humiliation.

His return to Rome near the end of June 46 BC was met with recognition for and much relief over what appeared to be a resolution of the civil war. The Senate had planned an unprecedented 40 days of public celebrations, commemorating Caesar's victories in Gaul (today's France), Egypt, Asia, and Africa. Some politicians, however, were still harboring resentment and fear.

Marcus Tullius Cicero, a well-respected statesman, lawyer, and philosopher, admired Caesar but was afraid of the dictator's unchecked power. *Alinari / Art Resource, NY*

Dictator

The critics' greatest concern had to do with Caesar's growing powers, which the Senate seemed ready to allow, confirming him first as consul (the highest title in the Roman republic), then as dictator for 10 years. He reached the height of his power in 44 BC, when he was given the title of dictator for life.

To his critics, this was a terrifying prospect. The Roman republic was meant to work through the Senate and other elected officials who held office for a short time. This system gave many people the chance to participate in the government and provided checks and balances to anyone in power. By accepting supreme powers for life, Caesar was moving very far from the republican ideal.

His personality didn't help. He was used to getting things done quickly and often made speedy decisions with little input from others, acting impatient with those who couldn't keep his pace. He seemed unfazed by his colleagues' fears. After all, he generally used his powers for the good of the people, applying his endless energy toward needed social, political, and cultural reforms.

Mother Cleopatra

In Egypt, Cleopatra enjoyed a time of relative peace. The Alexandrians and their rulers must have learned valuable lessons of peaceful coexistence, and Caesar's armies remaining in the region stood as a powerful reminder that internal squabbles and rebellions would be met with force.

It's hard to say if Caesar and Cleopatra missed each other, but Caesar continued to live up to his reputation as a ladies' man by having a short affair with a North African queen. It wasn't for nothing that his soldiers sang a teasing song warning people to lock up their wives at his arrival.

It is quite possible that Cleopatra had romantic feelings for Caesar. The Roman leader had saved her from either death or exile and restored her to power. In any case, he apparently left her a permanent reminder of their relationship—Cleopatra, now in her early 20s, was pregnant with a son.

The year of the child's birth is unknown, but it seems to have been around 47 or 46 BC. Following her family's tradition, she named him Ptolemy, adding Caesar as his second name. The people of Alexandria, always fond of nicknames, called him Caesarion, "little Caesar."

Historians aren't completely certain that the boy was Caesar's son, but the report was widespread and neither Caesar nor Cleopatra contested it. Only a few contrasting comments survive, including second-century historian Cassius Dio's suggestion that Cleopatra only pretended Caesarion was Caesar's son. According to Mark Antony, however, Caesar publicly recognized that he was the father.

As for the people of Egypt, they were not fussy when it came to their pharaohs. Cleopatra's father, Auletes, for example, had been recognized as king even though the people openly considered him an illegitimate son. Besides, living in a country with no prescribed wedding ceremonies, Cleopatra might have seen herself as Caesar's wife even

WHAT CAESAR LEARNED IN EGYPT

Some of Caesar's reforms show how his time in Egypt influenced him. For example, he planned the building of a public library very similar to the one he had seen in Alexandria and placed a renowned scholar in charge of collecting Latin and Greek literary works. Taking inspiration from the Alexandrian Museum, he also granted citizenship to any scholar who wanted to teach in Rome.

One of the best-known reforms he took from Egypt was the reorganization of the calendar with the help of the Alexandrian astronomer Sosigenes. In Rome a year consisted of 355 days. This calendar, originally based on the cycle of the moon, was obviously faulty and had to be constantly changed to keep pace with the seasons. Caesar's calendar (today known as the Julian calendar) used a variation of the 365-day Egyptian solar calendar (the oldest in the Mediterranean world) and added an extra day every few years (initially every three years, which became four later, during Caesar Augustus's reign). This is still the basis of our modern calendar.

One major difference between the Julian and the Egyptian calendars is the subdivision of months into seasons. Egyptians divided their year neatly into three seasons of four 30-day months. The seasons were determined by the Nile. Akhet was the time of flooding, Peret the season of planting and growing after the waters receded, and Shemu the time of harvest. The remaining five days, which fell just before Akhet, marked a period of national holiday.

if Caesar and the Roman people would have never entertained such a thought.

At any rate, she enthusiastically embraced her new role as a mother. Whoever the father,

she had produced an heir to the Egyptian throne and devoted her energies to caring for her child's health, education, and well-being.

This is evident in a bronze coin she issued in the Egyptian province of Cyprus: She is shown as a mother nursing her infant while holding a scepter and wearing a typical Hellenistic crown. On the back, the coin shows the double **cornucopia**, a horn-shaped container that is a symbol of everlasting fertility, and a Greek inscription: "Cleopatra the Queen."

In those days without mass media, coins were the best means of spreading royal news and political propaganda. Everyone used them, and no one threw them away. Since very few people had a chance to ever see their ruler, coins circulated the portrayal of each ruler and the message he or she chose to promote. On this coin, the message was clear: there was a new heir to the Egyptian throne.

Despite the image on the coin, Cleopatra probably didn't breast-feed her son, because both Egyptian and Greek mothers of high social status preferred to hire wet nurses to perform this time-consuming task. The image simply indicated that she was caring for Caesarion.

Following an Egyptian tradition, she either built or adapted a birth house in the Temple of Montu at Armant, about 12 miles south of Thebes. For Egyptians, birth houses (known as *mammisi*) were not places where mothers went to give birth. They were small portions of larger temples and were meant as commemorations of the birth of a pharaoh. Cleopatra dedicated her son's birth house to the god Harpre (Horus-the-Sun), protector of kings, whose birth was connected to both the daily rising of the sun and the periodic rise of a new pharaoh.

A Roman Villa for an Egyptian Queen

Cleopatra arrived in Rome in the fall of 46 BC, together with her brother Ptolemy XIV, her son Caesarion, and their entourage. She must have felt some uneasiness, given that Caesar had just paraded through the city displaying huge maps and illustrations of the Nile and the Alexandrian lighthouse as part of his conquests and bringing along Arsinoe as one of his prisoners.

After such a display, Cleopatra's arrival was met with a mixture of surprise, curiosity, criticism, fear, and outright hatred. Caesar hosted a party for her in one of his villas, surrounded by rich gardens just beyond the Tiber River, increasing rumors of their romance. Some said he wanted to divorce his wife, Calpurnia, with whom he had no children, in order to marry Cleopatra. According to others, he wanted to pass a new law allowing him to have as many wives as he liked. These rumors might have caused no concern in other nations, but the Roman republic was built on strict moral values, even if they were rapidly crumbling.

Other fears were more political in nature. How closely was Caesar working with Egypt? Was he planning to join East and West, like Alexander the Great had begun to do, and move the capital to Alexandria? What would that mean for the people of Rome?

As long as Cleopatra was in Egypt, rumors and fears were contained, but her presence in Rome definitely made many Romans uncomfortable. "[Caesar] incurred the greatest censure from all because of his passion for Cleopatra," Dio wrote, "not now the passion he had displayed in Egypt (for that was a matter of hearsay), but that which was displayed in Rome itself."

According to Dio, Caesar "was not at all concerned, however, about this, but actually enrolled them among the friends and allies of the Roman people," which was probably the reason for Cleopatra's visit.

One of the queen's fiercest opponents was the **statesman** Marcus Tullius Cicero, who found her arrogant, insolent, and a corrupting influence on Caesar. His judgment stemmed partially from a personal offense he had received. She had promised him some literary works that, in his view, were suitable to his status, but she broke her promise. There must have been more to it, because he couldn't even think back on that occasion without feeling pain.

There's no recorded response by Cleopatra, but if this was her first trip to Rome, she must have been puzzled by Caesar's tolerance for people who openly opposed and criticized him. That's not how things were done in Egypt.

Records show that she was in Rome in 44 BC, but it's unlikely that she stayed for two consecutive years. After all, Egypt was just recovering from a very unstable situation that had been partially caused by her father's prolonged residence in Rome. She probably visited Rome twice. According to Egyptologist Joyce Tyldesley, the first might

A depiction of Caesar's soldiers carrying trophies in triumph. Besides precious spoils, the soldiers are carrying pieces of defeated enemies' armor. *National Gallery of Art, Rosenwald Collection*

SOLVE EGYPTIAN MATH PROBLEMS

By the time Cleopatra became queen, the Ptolemies had already established a sophisticated banking system, with a central bank in Alexandria. Until the New Kingdom (1550–1069 BC), however, Egyptians didn't have paper or coin currency. They used bartering, exchanging one good for another, and scribes and merchants had to learn to calculate the proper exchange.

When it came to fractions, Egyptians had complicated rules. They never used numerators (the top number in a fraction) higher than 1 (except in ⅔ and ¾) and were not allowed to repeat a fraction in the same addition. For example, what if you were an ancient Egyptian and had to divide 6 loaves of bread among 10 people? You can't say that each person will get $\frac{6}{10}$ of a loaf, since the numerator is higher than 1. You have to reduce $\frac{6}{10}$ to an addition where all the numerators are 1. Try using $\frac{1}{10}$ as your first fraction. What's left? $\frac{6}{10} - \frac{1}{10} = \frac{5}{10}$, which is equivalent to ½. So you can say that each person will get ½ loaf of bread (using up five of the loaves), plus $\frac{1}{10}$ of the sixth loaf. As you see, it's more practical than cutting up ten loaves into ten equal parts and giving six of these parts to each person.

1. Try your hand at it: What if now you had to divide 7 loaves among 10 people? Follow the same process in the paragraph above. If you are having trouble, check your answer here: https://nrich.maths .org/1173.

2. Now that you understand the principle, create some simple math problems for your friends.

If you have not yet studied fractions, here is a simplified version of problem 65 of the Rhind Papyrus (an ancient Egyptian mathematical text): If you had to divide 130 loaves among 10 people, including a boatman, a foreman, and a door keeper who each receive double portions, what would be the share received by each person? (Clue: If you are having a hard time, count the portions, not the people.)

Answers: step 1: $\frac{5}{10} + \frac{2}{10}$, which is equivalent to ½ + $\frac{1}{5}$. So each person will get half a loaf, using up five of the loaves, plus $\frac{1}{5}$ of a loaf, which uses up the remaining two loaves.

problem 65: Count the portions. The boatman, foreman, and door keeper get one portion each (6 portions total). The other seven people get two portions each (7 portions total). 7 + 6 = 13 portions. Now you have to find out how many loaves are in a portion. 130 loaves ÷ 13 portions = 10 loaves. Each person gets 10 loaves, except the boatman, the foreman, and the door keeper, who get 20.

have been a more official visit, with her brother, to gain the status of "friends and allies of the Roman people," and the second one "with or without Ptolemy, to discuss the future of Egypt and Cyprus."

In any case, she was there on March 15, 44 BC, when the unexpected happened.

Death and Flight

Late that morning, Caesar attended a Senate meeting despite a series of bad **omens** (warnings) and his wife's insistence that he not go, as she had just dreamed about his death. Mark Antony, who had been Caesar's right-hand man for years and was consul with him at that time, accompanied him to the entrance of the meeting place—Pompey's Theatre, in the center of Rome. Before they could enter, however, Antony was called aside by a fellow politician who asked to speak to him privately. In reality, it was a ploy to keep him away from Caesar.

As soon as Caesar entered the theater, everyone stood to greet him. One senator approached him with a petition to sign, but Caesar, eager to get to the meeting's main issues, dismissed him. Pretending great distress, the senator grabbed Caesar's toga begging for attention, while others pressed against Caesar from all sides. Once they had him surrounded, one senator began to stab him and others rushed in. In the confusion, some ended up wounding each other. Everything happened so fast that Caesar's supporters couldn't do anything to help.

At this point, Caesar had a now famous encounter with Marcus Junius Brutus, a young senator he had loved as a son. Shocked to see Brutus among his assassins, Caesar whispered in Greek, "You too, my child?" Those were his last words. He wrapped his face in his toga and died on the floor. In all, he had been stabbed 23 times.

When the news spread, the whole city went into general panic. Who would be the next victim? Caesar's supporters dreaded a large-scale attack, while his opponents feared retaliation. Even Cicero, who had been an outspoken defender of the republic, was caught by surprise by this unexpected turn of events and ran for cover, ignoring

(left) **An artist's interpretation of Caesar's assassination.** *Heritage History, www.heritage-history.com*

(below) **Marcus Brutus.** *© RMN-Grand Palais / Art Resource*

51

Brutus's call to lead the people. The conspirators (a group of about 60 senators led by Brutus and his brother-in-law Gaius Cassius Longinus) had not made plans for the aftermath of their action.

Most everyone—politicians and common people—ran through the streets, seeking refuge behind bolted doors. Antony did the same, discarding his consular robe to avoid any attention as he rushed to barricade his house. Cleopatra might have hidden too, once again fearing for her life. Whatever her romantic feelings were for Caesar, she must have mourned a man who had been so close to her in many ways—her greatest political ally and the father of her child.

She had already been preparing to return home because Caesar had been about to leave for a new military campaign. Instead, she stayed another month. Initially a locked home was safer than the road, where robbers or assassins could work freely in the chaos. She might also have tried to secure her formal alliance with Rome by waiting to see who rose to power and making sure they were willing to respect previous agreements. In this case, her decision to stay at such a dangerous time showed courage and determination.

Caesar's funeral was held on March 20, attracting a large and diverse crowd from all over Rome, other parts of Italy, and neighboring countries. Many people had loved and respected Caesar as an exceptional general, an intelligent statesman, and a generous leader. Moved by grief, they threw robes, jewelry, and weapons in the fire that burned his body. Instead of ending, the worship of Caesar was just taking wing.

Later Caesar's will was formally read. The dictator had left his large gardens near the Tiber to the people of Rome and to each Roman a sum of money equivalent to one-third of a legionnaire's annual pay.

Since neither Calpurnia nor his previous wives had left him any sons, in his will Caesar had adopted his 18-year-old great-nephew Gaius Octavius (also known as Octavian) as his son and made him heir of three-fourths of his estate. The other fourth was left to two friends. Caesar's son with Cleopatra, Caesarion, was not mentioned. This was not surprising. Roman laws forbade leaving inheritance to noncitizens. What was surprising was the absence of Antony in the will, given that he had been Caesar's faithful right-hand man for a good part of ten years. Antony was undoubtedly hurt and stunned.

Ruling Solo

The atmosphere in Rome became particularly unsafe after Caesar's funeral, which had fueled the fury of Caesar's supporters. Quite certainly, Cleopatra arranged to leave as soon as her status of friend and ally of the Roman people was reconfirmed. By mid-April she was no longer in Rome.

Soon after her departure, Ptolemy XIV died of unknown causes. There were rumors that Cleopatra had killed him. The Roman-Jewish historian Titus Flavius Josephus, writing shortly after her death, had no doubts about it. "She was also by nature very covetous [greedy]," he wrote, "and stuck at no wickedness. She . . . poisoned her brother, because she knew that he was to be King of Egypt, and this when he was but fifteen years old."

Josephus, who drew much of his information from Nicolaus of Damascus, a tutor hired by Cleopatra, had a negative opinion of the queen. His views, however, were not too far-fetched. According to Tyldesley, Ptolemy XIV might have remained in Egypt during Cleopatra's second visit to Rome and tried to assume total power. In that scenario, she would have killed him as a rebel.

In any event, whether Ptolemy was murdered, executed, or died from other causes, Cleopatra benefited from this turn of events. With no other heir present in Egypt to claim the throne, the young Caesarion was officially crowned pharaoh under the name Ptolemy XV Theos Philopator Philometor (Father-Loving, Mother-Loving God), with Cleopatra ruling on his behalf while he was underage—a common scenario in ancient Egypt.

Cleopatra quickly took advantage of this new arrangement, identifying herself with the Egyptian mother-goddess Isis, who had become the power behind her son, Horus, after the death of her husband, Osiris. There were many parallels between Cleopatra and Isis: They were both single mothers, and both of their sons' fathers had been murdered—one by a brother and the other by dear friends. Like Isis, Cleopatra had taken charge of her situation and was raising her son to rule.

The similarities between Cleopatra and Isis are highlighted on an Armant birth house wall, in an inscription that describes the queen as "the female Horus, the great one, mistress of perfection,

A sculpture of Isis nursing her son, Horus. *The Walters Art Museum, Baltimore*

brilliant in counsel, Mistress of the Two Lands, Cleopatra, the goddess who loves her father." Some drawings on the inner walls showed two identical cow-headed goddesses breast-feeding their babies. One of the little ones might have represented Caesarion, because the walls are full of inscriptions with his name. Since Isis was often portrayed as

MAKE AN EGYPTIAN-STYLE WIG

Due to the hot climate, many people in Egypt shaved their heads or cut their hair very short. Children and priests kept their heads shaven. Sometimes children had just a long side-lock of hair. Other people wore wigs for special occasions or to keep their heads warm at night.

In the image of Isis nursing her son, Isis wears a tripartite (three-part) wig, which was proper for goddesses and queens. Tripartite wigs were composed of three distinct parts joined together. One part fell on one side of the head, another part on the other side, and the third part behind. The most expensive wigs were made of human hair. Palm fibers and wool were also used.

You can make a tripartite wig out of yarn.

MATERIALS

- Measuring tape
- 1 skein of bulky black yarn, about 87 yards
- Corrugated cardboard or thin book, about the same length or width as the distance from the top of your head to your shoulder
- Scissors
- Chalk (optional)
- Black knit or crocheted beanie
- Safety pin
- Crochet hook

1. Measure the distance from the top of your head to your shoulder.

2. Wrap all the yarn around a piece of cardboard or thin book measuring about the same length or width as your head-to-shoulder measurement. Then cut through the yarn on one side. Line up the yarn pieces.

3. Mark a straight line with chalk from the top of the beanie to the bottom edge.

4. Try the hat on, keeping the line in the front. If the hat covers your forehead, fold up the edge until your forehead is visible (tripartite wigs didn't include bangs) and the hat fits snugly. Take off the hat and pin the fold with a safety pin so it stays in place while you're working. Redraw the chalk line on the fold if needed.

5. Push your crochet hook from the inside of the hat through the top point of the beanie, staying close to but on one side of the chalk line. Pick up one end of a piece of yarn with the hook and pull it halfway through.

6. Hold the yarn tail on the outside of the hat. Push the hook back through the top of the hat from the outside, on the other side of the line, as close as possible to the first hole and pick up the other yarn tail from inside the hat. Pull it through.

7. Repeat steps 5 and 6, moving from the top of the hat to the bottom edge until the line is covered (it should take about 12–15 pieces of yarn, leaving 5–6 for the back).

8. Turn the hat so the back is toward you, and push the yarn forward.

9. Draw a 5-inch horizontal chalk line just below the top of the hat. This will be where the back portion of your wig starts.

10. Push your crochet hook through the hat from the inside at one end of your horizontal line. Pick up a yarn piece on the hook and pull it halfway through.

11. As in step 6, hold the yarn tail outside the hat and push the hook through the top of the hat as close as possible to the first hole on the same horizontal line. Hook the yarn tail inside the hat and pull it through so that both halves are poking out of the hat.

12. Repeat steps 10–11 across the horizontal line.

13. Fit the hat on your head and arrange the yarn "hair" so it's even.

EGYPTIAN GODS

Like most people from the nations around them (with the exception of Israel), Egyptians worshiped many gods—one or more for each aspect of life. Many were connected to particular places.

These divinities were said to look like humans or a mixture of humans and animals, with feelings and emotions that changed unpredictably from time to time. When something terrible happened, people thought the gods were angry and offered sacrifices to appease them.

These gods and goddesses could change in importance and assume new roles in different places or times. Egyptians believed they mostly lived in sanctuaries that were erected in their honor, where the priests cared for their statues day and night as parents care for a child, washing them, dressing them, and offering them food daily.

Contrary to popular opinion, Egyptians didn't worship animals, with the exception of two bulls—the Apis bull in Lower Egypt (the northern area around the Nile delta), and the Buchis bull in Upper Egypt (south)—which were raised and pampered as gods in temples built for this purpose. When one of these bulls died, it was mummified and buried as a god while Egyptians looked for the bull that was supposed to take its place (they had special birthmarks).

Some gods, however, were thought to occasionally take the form of animals, so these animals eventually became protected. During Auletes's reign, an angry mob murdered a Roman when he accidentally killed a cat.

You can find an illustrated list of Egyptian gods at the website Discovering Ancient Egypt here: http://discoveringegypt.com/ancient-egyptian-gods-and-goddesses.

a cow or with a cow's head, the images gave the message that Isis and Cleopatra were identical—Cleopatra was the new Isis.

Cleopatra's images on temple walls were essential because pharaohs were considered the only effective link between the people and the gods. In theory, only the pharaohs could communicate with the gods, bring them offerings, and intercede for the people. In reality, pharaohs couldn't be in all temples at once, so the priests could legitimately take their place for everyday worship. At the same time, just like the images in the tombs represented the deceased's life in the next world, images of pharaohs on temple walls served as substitutes for the rulers' actual presence.

The work on the Dendera relief, planned or at least approved by Cleopatra in cooperation with the temple priests, was performed mostly after her death, a reminder for generations of worshipers of the queen's devotion to her son.

CREATE AN EGYPTIAN RELIEF SCULPTURE

*Egyptian **reliefs** and sculptures followed many of the same strict rules as Egyptian paintings. Reliefs are divided into raised and sunken forms. In a raised relief, the figures are higher than the surface. In a sunken relief, their outlines are carved into the surface. This activity will teach you how to make a sunken relief, like the ones found in the temple at Dendera.*

MATERIALS

- Rolling pin (optional)
- ½ pound air-drying modeling clay
- Paper
- Pencil
- Plastic modeling tools

1. Using a rolling pin, flatten ½ pound of air-drying modeling clay until it is about ¼ inch thick.

2. On a piece of paper at least as big as your flattened clay, draw the picture you want to carve. This will help you get an idea of the size and proportions. Remember the rules you learned in the "Draw and Color Like an Ancient Egyptian" activity on page 44.

3. Using a thin modeling tool, press lightly to draw your image on the clay, looking at your paper drawing for reference. If you make a mistake, rub your hand gently over the clay surface to erase it and try again.

4. Once you are satisfied with your clay image, trace it with the same modeling tool, pressing harder.

5. Trim the clay around your picture to form a neat geometrical shape (rectangle, square, circle, oval, etc.).

6. Let the clay dry according to the instructions on the package.

If you want to make a raised relief, after step 4 scrape away the clay around the image until the image stands out.

Cleopatra and Mark Antony

Captivated by love for Cleopatra, [Antony] restored himself in her embrace as if his affairs were well in order. —Lucius Annaeus Florus

Any politician who thought 18-year-old Octavian could be easily manipulated was in for a surprise. Behind his baby face was a mind as shrewd, ambitious, and focused as his great-uncle's and quick to seize any opportunity that came his way. Octavian was also self-confident and handsome—two traits that charmed many people around him.

The Viceroy's Boat, from the tomb of Amenhotep Huy (ca. 1353–1327 BC).
Wikimedia Commons/Metropolitan Museum of Art

A New Civil War

Forty-year-old Antony, who saw himself as Caesar's more logical successor, found himself surprisingly outplayed. The competition between Octavian and him developed into an actual armed conflict, which would have continued if an imminent threat hadn't forced them to unite. Two prominent conspirators of Caesar's death, Brutus and his friend Gaius Cassius Longinus, had moved east to increase their military and financial resources in order to fight for the restoration of the republic. To reinforce their counterattack, Octavian and Antony enlisted the help of another close ally of Julius Caesar, Marcus Aemilius Lepidus, forming a league called a **triumvirate**, or group of three.

It was not a new idea. In 60 BC Julius Caesar, Pompey, and Marcus Licinius Crassus had formed a first triumvirate as an unofficial group of like-minded politicians. This time, however, Antony, Lepidus, and Octavian obtained the Senate's approval and assumed executive powers. Soon they started to act as dictators, making decisions without consulting either the Senate or the people.

In a radical departure from Caesar's policy of forgiveness, they posted a list of Caesar's enemies in the Forum and promised a reward to anyone who killed them. The list eventually surpassed 2,000 names, including those of men who opposed the triumvirate. Some managed to flee, but many, like Cicero, lost their lives. After their executions, the triumvirs, or ruling trio,

seized their goods and used the money to pay their armies.

Finally, in 42 BC, once their forces were sufficiently manned and supplied, Antony and Octavian left Lepidus in Rome and led their separate troops east to deal with Brutus and Cassius. On October 2 they arrived in the plain of Philippi, in eastern Macedonia, where the two conspirators had already camped. A fierce battle began, with Antony bearing the brunt of both organization and action because Octavian had arrived to the camp severely ill.

A Difficult Choice

In that tense situation, Cleopatra received many requests for military and economic support. Already at the start of 43 BC, Cornelius Publius Dolabella, a Roman **proconsul** (a high elected magistrate) who had switched sides from the republicans to the triumvirs, had asked her to send him the legions Caesar had left in Egypt.

She readily agreed. In some ways, this request must have been a relief. Those Roman legions were, at that time, a mighty, highly sought-after force of fighting men, and many requests would have certainly followed. By sending them off to a Roman official, Cleopatra could say she was obeying a rightful authority. Besides, General Dolabella was fighting against the assassins of the father of her child.

In the end, Cassius intercepted her legions, took them over, and defeated Dolabella. This put Cleopatra in a very difficult spot. What if Cassius

Marcus Aemilius Lepidus on a Roman coin. In the triumvirate with Antony and Octavian, Lepidus was in charge of Rome's North African provinces. In 36 BC Octavian found a reason to exclude him from the triumvirate. *Classical Numismatic Group, Inc., www.cngcoins.com*

and Brutus, strengthened by this victory, decided to turn against her for supporting their enemy? Apparently Cassius twice threatened to invade Egypt and replace her with her sister Arsinoe, whom Caesar had confined to the Temple of Artemis at Ephesus. It was within his power to do it, since Ephesus was now under his control. Without Roman legions, Cleopatra was left with a small mercenary army that was barely sufficient to resolve national problems.

For the time being, however, Cassius and Brutus kept busy with the war and simply asked Cleopatra to send them other resources: money, grain, and warships. It was a difficult request for an undermanned queen without a strong political ally. In spite of any emotional ties to Caesar, her overarching goal was to stay in power. To that end, she didn't want to antagonize the potential winner of this conflict, but how could she predict the outcome? How could she avoid backing the losing side?

As she had done in similar situations, she decided to stall. She had pressing problems at home, she said. Finally, she decided to lead some warships to the battlefield, but not to help Cassius. She chose to back the triumvirs instead. It was a risky step. It's not clear how she planned to play out this move, but the sea decided for her, turning fiercely against her in a life-threatening storm that forced her to retreat, bringing home a badly battered fleet. On top of it, she became gravely ill.

Undeterred, Cleopatra ordered the repair of her warships and the construction of new ones. It was going to be costly, especially in the suffering

EGYPTIAN SHIPS

The first Egyptian vessels were simple reed boats that were used to navigate the Nile. Over time, some of these boats became more sophisticated, adding room for sails and oarsmen. Wooden boats were a later addition, because few trees grow in Egypt and most of the wood had to be imported, especially from Lebanon or Cyprus.

For much of Egyptian history, warships were used mostly to defend the coasts or transport material to the battleground. By the time Cleopatra was queen, however, the ships were already very similar to those used in Greece or Rome and were employed in actual sea warfare.

Carving of an ancient Roman battleship with soldiers, first century BC. © Vanni Archive/ Art Resource, NY

Model of an ancient Egyptian boat, from the Tomb of Pharaoh Tutankhamen (c.1332–1323 BC), Egypt, 18th Dynasty. The body of the ship is carved from a single log. Borromeo / Art Resource, NY

BUILD A SHADOOF

To bring water from a river or pond to a higher field, Egyptians used the shadoof, a tool based on a simple **lever**. To get an idea of how this worked, build a similar tool using items around your home.

MATERIALS

- Plastic drop cloth (optional)
- 5-by-10-by-5-inch box
- 2 small bowls
- Water
- 3 pencils with erasers
- Hair elastic
- 16-inch piece of strong thread or string
- Bottle cap from a 24-ounce Arrowhead Sport Cap water bottle (or bottle with identical cap)
- Knitting needle or Afghan crochet hook
- Tape

1. Protect your work surface with a plastic drop cloth. Put a box that's about 5 by 10 inches and 5 inches high on the work surface.

2. Fill one of two small bowls with water and place it next to the box.

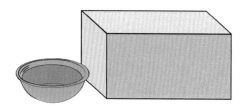

3. Hold the three pencils together all going the same direction. Wrap an elastic hair band three times around them about 1½ inches from the lead end, then one more time around one pencil only.

4. Move the eraser ends of the pencils apart from one another so that you form a tripod, with the eraser ends as the legs.

5. Place the pencil tripod on the box. The erasers will keep the tripod from sliding.

6. Place another small, empty bowl on the box in front of the tripod (between the bowl of water and the tripod).

7. Tie one end of a 16-inch piece of strong thread or string tightly around one of the two "handles" of the bottle cap. Tie the other end of the thread to the second handle.

8. Wrap the middle of the string once around the dull end of a knitting needle. Make sure the two sides of the string are even. Then secure the string to the needle with a small piece of tape.

9. Position the center of the knitting needle on the pencil tripod so that the bottle cap, or "bucket," hangs over the bowl of water. Raise the sharp end of the needle to let the bucket drop into the water until it is full.

10. Now gently pull down the sharp end of the needle, moving the water-filled bucket up from the bowl.

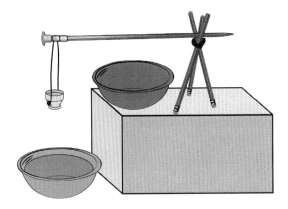

11. Move the needle back until the bucket is above the empty bowl. Then lower the bucket by raising the sharp end of the needle and empty the water into the bowl. Repeat as many times as you like.

In a field, one worker would operate the lever and another would empty the bucket.

Egyptian economy. The Nile had not flooded that summer, and the dry fields had not produced food. This had caused famine, illness, and rebellion. She couldn't afford to remain idle though. Her place on the throne depended on Rome, and when Rome called, she had to answer. The threat of being replaced by Arsinoe continued to loom.

As it turned out, she never had to join the battle. After a fierce struggle, Antony and Octavian won an overwhelming victory and both Cassius and Brutus committed suicide—all before Cleopatra could even leave Egypt.

Although Antony and Octavian shared the victory, the soldiers saw Antony as the true winning leader, because 21-year-old Octavian had been virtually incapacitated by his illness. In fact, there were rumors that he was dying. After the victory, he was immediately taken back to Rome, while Antony remained in the east to encourage the troops, order the honorable disposal of Roman bodies, and sort out the situation in the provinces.

The victory at Philippi, the greatest in Antony's life, elevated him in the eyes of the people, who, grateful for the ensuing peace, saw him as Caesar's true successor. Even Brutus's and Cassius's troops recognized him as their leader. He was the winning star Cleopatra had been awaiting.

A Cinematic Appearance

The triumph motivated Antony to embark on a greatly anticipated venture: the conquest of Parthia—the same mission Julius Caesar had been about to undertake at the time of his assassination. The Parthians had become a major thorn in Rome's side, and Antony wanted to crush them for good and conquer their lands. In doing so, he would secure his place as the dictator's true successor.

It was then, in the summer of 41, that Antony called Cleopatra to the city of Tarsus (in today's Turkey), with the purpose of clarifying her position and allegiance. Why had her governor in Cyprus backed Cassius, and why had she promised to send Cassius warships and supplies? Was she still faithful to Caesar and his men, or had she turned to his murderers' side? He must have anticipated how Cleopatra would answer. Given the triumvirs' victory, she would have been foolish to oppose them. To free herself from suspicion, she would be wise to supply the funds they needed.

What he didn't expect was her procrastination, in spite of repeated reminders. According to Plutarch, she carefully planned her response, taking to heart the recommendation of Antony's messenger, who, noticing the queen's beauty and intelligence, suggested a strategy.

First of all, he said, Cleopatra should not "be afraid of Antony, who was the most agreeable and humane of commanders." What she should do, given his master's passion for splendor, women, and wine, was meet him "decked out in fine array."

Cleopatra would have immediately recognized that expression as a reference to Homer's *Iliad*, one of the bestselling poems of her times. The quote referred to a meeting between the goddess Hera and Zeus, head of the Greek gods. Hera engineered the meeting to turn the tide of the Trojan War and in Homer's story went to great lengths to charm the god, involving other goddesses in her elaborate plans.

Cleopatra rose to the task. In spite of her country's dire financial condition, she spared no expense and commissioned the building of a luxurious

Cleopatra's barge, from a 19th-century painting by Hans Makart.
Nicoolay, iStock

barge with a golden **stern**, silver-plated oars, and purple sails. She then filled it with all sorts of expensive and impressive treasures. Rome's support was well worth the sacrifice. Finally, she set sail, followed by other boats heavy with workers and supplies.

During the last portion of her trip, she positioned herself on the deck of the barge under a gold-embroidered canopy, robed as Aphrodite, the Greek goddess of love. All around her, slave boys dressed as **cupids** fanned her while beautiful female slaves, clothed as mythological sea **nymphs**, stood by the rudders and ropes.

The boat slowly approached its destination, shining in the sun and attracting astonished crowds. At her command, the loud music of flutes and harps overpowered the quiet swishing of the water against the hull and the smoke of incense engulfed the boat, so much that it could be smelled from shore.

At the news, Antony rushed to the river, while the people, always ready to turn their leaders into gods, passed the word that Aphrodite had come to party with Dionysus "for the good of Asia"—an announcement that was sure to please the extravagant Roman. It was not the first time that he was associated with the god of wine. When he entered Ephesus after the Philippian war, he was greeted by a cheering crowd who hailed him as "Dionysus Giver of Joy and Goods."

To Cleopatra, the imagery must have brought back memories of her father, who had added "New Dionysus" to his name and celebrated in full splendor the yearly festivities for the Greek god.

Dionysus, the Greek god of wine.
The Walters Art Museum, Baltimore

Following the customary etiquette, Antony sent a messenger to invite Cleopatra for dinner. The greater of two people would usually extend the first invitation and, as a Roman, Antony naturally considered himself the greater. Cleopatra was of a different mind. Reversing the roles, she suggested he join her instead. In fact, she had already planned an extraordinary banquet on her boat.

Antony accepted the invitation. When he entered the boat that evening, he was immediately dumbstruck at the brightness of the place. A "multitude of lights"—probably clusters of lamps—hung everywhere, "arranged and ordered with so many inclinations and adjustments to each other in the form of rectangles and circles."

The quantity of food was equally astonishing. A feast was served on golden plates decorated with precious stones, in a room filled with golden and purple hangings. After the meal, Cleopatra gave plates and cups to Antony and his men to keep, much like we do with party favors. The next evening, Antony tried to reciprocate, but his servants couldn't even come close to the lavishness and magnificence of the queen's table and entertainment.

The third evening, she served an even more spectacular meal on more precious plates and gave those away too. This time she also gave Antony and his officials the couches on which they had been reclining, providing some litters with bearers to take them home. For all the other visitors, she provided horses, while Ethiopian slaves carried torches to light the way for everyone. On the fourth evening, she arranged for a shower of rose petals to fall onto the guests, to a depth of 1½ feet.

These accounts seem almost fictional, but extravagance and splendor were very common with ancient monarchs and particularly with the Ptolemies. It's also possible that the stories have been embellished over time. In any case, they give a good idea of Cleopatra's resourcefulness and the Ptolemies' willingness to go to any length to stay in power.

In the end, Cleopatra succeeded in impressing Antony and firmly attaching him to her cause. Her luxury gave a reassuring message: in spite of the recent low tides and ensuing economic problems, Egypt was still a rich country.

A New Alliance

While these lavish scenes have most captured history's attention, the two leaders did more than party. They seriously discussed the future of their countries and their continued alliance.

Cleopatra was well prepared to answer Antony's questions about her loyalty to Rome. When she had sent four legions to General Dolabella, he was on Antony's side. Later, in spite of Cassius's threats, she had prepared an impressive fleet to deliver to the triumvirs. Each time, her plans were foiled, first by the interception of her legions and then by an unbeatable storm, by no fault of her own.

The explanation must have convinced Antony, who moved on to other issues. Like Caesar, it was in Antony's best interest to keep Egypt running independently. Over the years, Cleopatra had seemed to manage her country well, and her joint rule with her son, Caesarion, promised stability. As long as she was willing to provide support to Antony, he was willing to keep her on the throne.

The queen, however, had a request of her own—one that might have put Antony's commitment to the test: kill her exiled sister, Arsinoe. Cleopatra was tired of threats and the ever-present danger and uncertainty that came with power. The chaotic state of Roman affairs encouraged new political alliances, and the idea that Cleopatra's sister could find powerful backing was not far-fetched. It had happened often enough.

As horrifying as this sounds, the practice of killing political enemies and rivals was common at that time. In fact, a similar execution had already happened in Egypt when a young man had the unwise idea of presenting himself as the long-lost Ptolemy XIII, saying he had survived the boat wreck and had been living in exile. Cleopatra took no chances.

Antony agreed. In some ways, Arsinoe's death was to his benefit anyway, as removing the threat of a rival to Cleopatra provided the stability in Egypt he desired.

By the end of their meeting, he and Cleopatra had become lovers, and this union cemented their political alliance.

The Inimitables

Antony moved to Cleopatra's palace for the winter, when navigation and wars were normally suspended. Unlike Caesar, he didn't enter Alexandria as a Roman leader. Instead, he lived as a civilian, wearing an informal Greek tunic and blending in with the Greek community, who readily accepted him. With other like-minded friends, the two lovers started a society called the Inimitables, a circle of people who could live it up like no others. Every night, they met to eat, drink, and play games, including games of dice, a favorite Roman pastime.

On some nights Antony, a lover of pranks, went out dressed as a common slave, playing tricks on people and even peeking into houses. Most of the time, the Alexandrians played along, but occasionally they beat him and sent him home with bruises.

Apparently Cleopatra went along and joined him in disguise, dressed as a maid. In fact, Plutarch says she kept an eye on him day and night, to keep him either out of trouble or close to her.

Antony made even Cleopatra the target of his practical jokes, so she did the same with him. Once he tried to convince her he was a great fisherman by sending a man to place a fish on his hook. He repeated the trick two or three times. Cleopatra, aware of the hoax, pretended to believe him and encouraged him to show his talents to others. The next day, she invited a large company of people to join them on boats. At the same time, she made

A board used to play mehen, an ancient Egyptian game. *Daderot, Wikimedia Commons*

MAKE A MEHEN BOARD

Cleopatra might have shown Antony how to play Egyptian games like senet or mehen. Senet boards and pieces are readily available today, with fairly accurate rules. Archaeologists are not sure how mehen was played though. It might have been similar to the board game Chutes and Ladders, also known generically as snakes and ladders in many countries. It involved a board shaped like a coiled snake. Some small figurines (mostly lions) and marbles have also been found next to the board in some Egyptian tombs.

You can make your own simple mehen board from clay.

MATERIALS

- 1 pound air-drying modeling clay
- Plastic modeling tools

1. On a clean table, with both palms, roll a portion of modeling clay into a snake shape about ½ inch thick.

2. Wrap the snake gently around itself to form a coil. It should turn about 4–5 times around itself. If you need to add another snake, follow step 1 and then connect the new snake to the old one by kneading the end pieces gently together.

3. Taper the outer end of the snake by rolling it thinner. Then secure this end by pressing it gently against the outer coil. This coiled snake is your board.

4. Using either a flat or thin plastic modeling tool, press gently between the coils to better define the space between them.

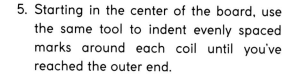

5. Starting in the center of the board, use the same tool to indent evenly spaced marks around each coil until you've reached the outer end.

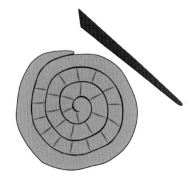

6. Now turn the board over. Use a flat modeling tool to smooth the bottom of the mehen board. If there are any gaps, the board will come apart after it dries.

7. Let the clay dry according to the instructions on the package.

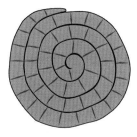

8. Make your own rules for how to play the game, or look online for ideas. For example, this site has a simple suggestion: https://traveltoeat.com/ancient-board-games-british-museum.

sure that one of her men could get in the water before Antony's helper and had him place a piece of dried, salted herring on Antony's hook. When Antony pulled up the line, there was a roar of laughter.

Plutarch, who told the story, included Cleopatra's remark to Antony: "**Imperator**, hand over your fishing-rod to the fishermen of Pharos and Canopus [an ancient Egyptian coastal city]; your sport is the hunting of cities, realms, and continents."

Besides fishing, Antony and Cleopatra enjoyed hunting, a sport that was very popular with the Macedonian upper class. She also watched him practice his fighting skills at the gymnasium and took him to attend lectures at the museum. Medieval Arab writers describe Cleopatra as a lover of philosophy, mathematics, and medicine who enjoyed spending time in the company of scholars, and Antony—a great enthusiast of Greek culture—must have admired her knowledge. There is no record of a Nile cruise this time, probably because Cleopatra's reign was already established and she didn't need to make a political statement to her people. Most likely she took Antony on tours of local or nearby attractions.

Meals, as usual, were extraordinary. Plutarch's grandfather passed on a story about a friend who, while visiting Cleopatra's kitchen, was astonished at the amount of food that was prepared, which included eight wild boars. He thought they were expecting a lot of company. Amused, the cooks replied it was for twelve people, but everything had to be perfect. If the food was not served on time,

it would spoil. Sometimes Antony ordered a meal and then put it off for a while, so the cooks prepared many dinners in order to be ready at any time.

Pliny the Elder, a first-century Roman author and scientist, added an account that became legendary: Cleopatra's claim that she could serve a meal worth 10,000,000 **sesterces** (enough money to buy a fancy villa). Antony, initially incredulous, laughed when she served him a meal that was elaborate but quite common for the queen. She told him to wait. There was still one course, and it was just for her.

A servant brought her a bowl of particularly strong vinegar. Taking off one of the expensive pearl earrings she had inherited from Oriental kings (the largest pearls ever discovered, according to Pliny), she dropped one in the vinegar. Once it was fully dissolved, she drank it.

The story is quite incredible. A pearl can dissolve in very strong vinegar (Egyptian vinegar was 8 percent acetic acid), but not instantly. There are, however, ways to speed up the chemical reaction (with heat or by adding other substances). Cleopatra, who seems to have been very interested in science, might have learned some of these techniques from books. She could have also consumed the pearl on a different night or dissolved it enough to allow her to swallow it whole. Whatever the case, the account increased the fame of her extravagant dinner parties.

DISSOLVE AN EGGSHELL

Pearls dissolve in an acidic solution because the acid reacts with calcium carbonate, their main component. Calcium carbonate is also the main component in eggshells. By dissolving an eggshell in vinegar, you can understand the concept behind Cleopatra's trick.

MATERIALS

➣ Egg (raw or hard-boiled)

➣ Clear drinking glass

➣ 1 cup distilled white vinegar

1. Carefully place a raw or hard-boiled egg in a clear drinking glass. Be gentle, especially if the egg is raw.

2. Pour the vinegar in the glass, until the egg is covered completely.

3. Leave the egg in the vinegar overnight. Check to see if the shell is completely dissolved. If not, leave it longer, checking periodically.

4. When the shell is dissolved, observe the change.

The bubbles you see while the eggshell is dissolving are carbon dioxide gas, which is released when the acetic acid breaks down the calcium carbonate.

6

Queen of Kings

An Alexandrian crowd collected to see the sons of Cleopatra.
—Constantine P. Cavafy

Antony and Cleopatra's fun and games eventually came to an end. As soon as navigation became easier, Antony left to take care of some urgent matters, leaving behind a newly pregnant Cleopatra.

Battles and Wives

One of these pressing matters was a Parthian attack on the Roman province of Syria. In spite of its urgency, however, Antony had to focus his attention on the aftermath of a failed military coup in Rome, led by none other than his wife, Fulvia, and his brother Lucius. The coup followed Octavian's plan to confiscate people's properties in order to pay hundreds of retiring veterans.

The Temple at Edfu is the largest and best preserved of all Ptolemaic temples. Its construction started around 237 BC and ended in 57 BC. *José Miguel, Flickr*

This 43 BC coin representing the winged Victory was apparently minted after the likeness of Fulvia. *Classical Numismatic Group, Inc., www.cngcoins.com*

Fulvia and Lucius, both influential in Rome, moved straight to armed conflict, raising soldiers to defend the many families' interests, including theirs. There might have been other motivations, such as political ambition and perhaps jealousy. Both Plutarch and Appian said that Fulvia was trying to draw Antony away from Cleopatra.

Convincing Antony's veterans to fight against a man who was, after all, trying to pay them, was not easy, but Fulvia and Lucius eventually succeeded by appealing to the soldiers' devotion to Antony, who had always been a generous and faithful leader, and by depicting Octavian as disloyal and ungrateful. To appeal to the veterans' emotions, they brought along the children Antony and Fulvia had together: Marcus Antonius Antyllus and Iullus Antonius, who were about six and five years old.

In the end, after a short-lived attack on Rome, their armies were besieged in Perusia (today's Perugia, Italy) and forced to surrender. Octavian pardoned Lucius but sent him to govern Spain, a safe distance from Rome, while Fulvia fled to Athens, Greece.

Antony rushed to meet his wife and scold her for worsening his relations with Octavian. The scolding might have been for show, to convince Octavian he had just discovered the ordeal. It's logical to think he didn't want a confrontation with Octavian, even though, if Fulvia had won, it would have obviously been to his benefit.

After Antony's harsh treatment, Fulvia became gravely ill. According to Appian, her illness was caused by some sort of depression over "Antony's reproaches." Some of her contemporaries said she "had become a willing victim of disease on account of the anger of Antony." Maybe she gave up the will to fight an illness or exposed herself to the elements. In any case, at 40 years of age, she died soon after his departure.

Fulvia had been Antony's third wife, a determined and assertive woman who, according to Plutarch, "took no thought for spinning or housekeeping." In fact, the historian blames her for teaching Antony "to obey women," preparing him for Cleopatra's manipulation. Whatever the truth, Fulvia's marriage to Antony had been deeply passionate to begin with and punctuated by good times and sincere expressions of love.

No one knows how Antony reacted to Fulvia's death. Politically speaking, it helped his relationship with Octavian because the two triumvirs could blame her for the rebellion. As was common in those days, they cemented their renewed unity with a marriage. In October 40, 43-year-old Antony wed Octavian's sister Octavia, who at age 29 had just become a widow. Octavian had a special love for his sister, who was beautiful, intelligent, and, in a violent and scandalous age, faithful, kind, and good. Plutarch called her "a wonder of a woman."

In spite of being a marriage of convenience, the union between Antony and Octavia seemed happy, and there is every indication that they loved each other. For a few years, Cleopatra disappeared from Antony's love life, even if he was aware of the birth of the twins he had fathered with the queen and kept informed of the political and economic situation in Egypt.

New coins were immediately issued: some showing the faces of Antony and Octavian and others showing Antony and his new wife. The mood was hopeful. Was the civil war finally over? The acclaimed Roman poet Virgil wrote of a golden age, supposedly inaugurated by the birth of a boy. He might have been thinking of the marriage between Antony and Octavia, the new symbol of peace. In reality, the couple later had only two daughters, born three years apart and both named Antonia (their family name—at that particular time in history, Roman women were not usually given a first name).

After spending almost a year in Italy, Antony moved back to Athens to continue his supervision of Rome's eastern regions, while Octavian oversaw Italy, Gaul, and Spain and Lepidus oversaw the North African provinces. Antony took Octavia with him, as either an expression of sincere love or a reminder to the people of the unity between him and Octavian—or as both.

Once again he enjoyed the cultured Greek lifestyle, wearing Greek clothes, attending lectures, enjoying the cuisine, and attending religious festivals. Octavia, who was well educated and well read, was undoubtedly able to keep up with her husband, even when her first daughter was born shortly after their arrival.

The Athenians responded enthusiastically, hailing the couple as "the Benevolent Gods" and Antony—once again—as "the new Dionysus." By the end of the winter, Antony returned to his Roman uniform while Octavia continued working hard to maintain good relations between her husband and her brother. This task became particularly difficult when Octavian failed to send Antony four legions he had promised to give him in exchange for 120 warships.

This broken promise felt especially disappointing when, at the end of 37 BC, the political situation in Parthia became unstable, opening the door for a Roman conquest—an opportunity Antony didn't want to miss. The Parthian cavalry had a reputation for launching sudden and fierce attacks, advancing and retreating at a remarkable speed and, in case of defeat, regrouping with very few losses. This tough war required a strong army.

As usual, wars started in the spring, but Antony took advantage of the winter months to prepare. To that end, he moved to Antioch, a large city in

(left) **Parthian rider.** *Erich Lessing / Art Resource, NY*

(below) **A 39 BC coin showing the heads of Antony and Octavia on one side and the god Dionysus flanked by serpents on the other.** *Classical Numismatic Group, Inc., www.cngcoins.com*

today's Turkey, where he summoned several leaders—including Cleopatra. She agreed to help him but in return asked for the Roman territories that had belonged to the Ptolemies two centuries earlier, at the height of their power, to be restored to Egypt: Crete, Cilicia, Nabataea, Judaea, Cyrenaica, Phoenicia, and Cyprus. (Rome had taken back Cyprus, probably after Cleopatra's governor backed Cassius.)

It was not an outrageous request. After all, Cleopatra had been a loyal **client ruler**, reigning over her territories while still officially under Rome's control and making sure that Rome benefited from her decisions. For example, Cilicia was rich in timber and Nabataea in tar, and both were needed to build ships, which in turn Rome could use to its benefit. Antony, however, conceded only in part: he gave her control of the islands of Cyprus and Crete but only portions of the other countries.

As expected, the meeting between the two leaders was not limited to politics. Apparently Cleopatra stayed for the winter, and the two had plenty of time to enjoy each other's company and talk about their lives and the progress of the children they had together: Alexander Helios (Sun) and Cleopatra Selene (Moon). After winter, Antony went on to war and Cleopatra traveled back home, stopping to visit her new territories on the way.

Through all this, Octavia was in Rome, heavily pregnant with the second Antonia. If she received news about Cleopatra's stay with Antony, there was nothing she could do. Roman women were painfully used to their husbands' infidelities.

A New Beginning

On her jubilant return to Alexandria, Cleopatra, then 33, proclaimed the start of a new era—the return to a larger, more prosperous Egyptian kingdom. It was a significant event. Conquering foreign lands and increasing Egypt's wealth had always been considered one of the greatest achievements of any pharaoh, something that invariably called for great celebrations.

Egyptians started a new calendar year with every new pharaoh, so the year from the beginning of September 37 to the end of August 36 was already Year 16 of Cleopatra. From then on, however, it was to be known as "Year 16 that is Year 1," with every passing year following the same pattern until Cleopatra's death.

Undoubtedly, Cleopatra's triumph had to do with much more than the simple reacquisition of lands. After a three-year absence from her life, Antony had acknowledged the twins as his children and had probably reassured her of his support. Cleopatra's future still depended on the Roman government's favor—a favor that, as she had learned at Caesar's death, could vanish at any time.

To celebrate, she issued a new silver coin, minted in Antioch, with her image on one side and Antony's on the other. Under her image, she inscribed, "Queen Cleopatra, the Younger Goddess," and under his, "Imperator and Triumvir." It's possible that, as might have been the case with Caesar, she considered herself married to Antony, especially since she was carrying their third child. In any case, the images on the coin communicated to the people of her larger kingdom that she was rightfully ruling them with Rome's approval and under Rome's supervision.

She now had abundant income from not only her newly acquired countries' products but also a considerable yearly rent she demanded from the kings of Judaea and Nabataea for use of the territories that they previously administered independently. Among her new ventures was the import of balsam shrubs from her territories in Judaea to be replanted in her country, with the intent of producing a profitable amount of incense for religious rituals and a valuable medicinal balm (known as balm of Gilead). She also worked on strengthening the economy by promoting trade with other countries as distant as India and Sri Lanka.

As a mother, she focused on giving all of her children a superior education and on building a solid support for their futures. Her new resources allowed her to strengthen her existing good relations with the influential Egyptian priests by supporting their work and maintaining the construction of temples, especially those her father started at Dendera and Edfu. Besides any religious significance, a good relation between pharaohs and priests had political and economic advantages, since many temples generated independent sources of income, both from offerings and from the products of their lands.

Friend and Accomplice

With larger territories came greater responsibilities, as Cleopatra became involved in many of her new regions' affairs. This was particularly true in Judaea, where she had already developed a political connection with King Herod I and a deep friendship with his mother-in-law, Alexandra.

At one point, when Herod's distrust of Alexandra became so evident that Alexandra began to fear for her life and that of her son, Cleopatra advised them to escape to Egypt. She might have suggested the method: by hiding in two coffins. The ingenious plan failed when Alexandra was betrayed by a servant.

Fearing Cleopatra's anger (which could translate into Antony's disapproval), Herod the Great, as he was known, pretended to forgive his fleeing family members. But soon after the event, Alexandra's son drowned in a swimming accident that, according to Josephus, Herod had engineered.

Cleopatra, who spoke both Hebrew and Aramaic (the languages spoken in Judaea), continued to oversee the situation at Herod's court, asking Antony to intervene and making frequent visits to the king, who, as a typical politician, welcomed her enthusiastically. After she left, however, Herod spread a rumor that she had flirted with him but he had resisted her charms. Given Cleopatra's plain loyalty to Antony, this seems unlikely. It could have been Herod's perception or a simple desire to brag.

Cleopatra the Consoler

In the meantime, Antony's war against the Parthians didn't go as planned. The Parthians found a perfect opportunity to attack when Antony, out of impatience, left his supply wagons behind

MAKE A CARTOUCHE BOOKMARK WITH YOUR EGYPTIAN NAME

*Pharaohs' names are often found written in **hieroglyphs** within oval shapes that symbolize protection. In the 18th century French scholar Jean-François Champollion called them **cartouches** (pronounced kar-TOOSH), the French word for gun **cartridges**. The Armant birth house was full of cartouches with Caesarion's name. Egyptian cartouches could be carved out of any material.*

You can imitate the cartouche in the photo by using paper and pencil.

MATERIALS

- Computer with internet access
- 2 sheets 8½-by-11-inch card-stock paper
- Computer printer
- Scissors
- Glue stick
- Tape
- Sharpened colored pencil

1. Use the Penn Museum website at www .penn.museum/cgi/hieroglyphsreal.php to find what your name is in hieroglyphs.

2. Click your mouse immediately after your name and drag it down to select the whole image.

3. Right-click on the selected image and select "Copy Image."

4. Open a blank document and paste the image by right-clicking in the document and selecting "Paste." If your name is long and runs onto a second page, try using a nickname.

5. Load one sheet of 8½-by-11-inch card-stock paper in your computer printer. Print a copy of the document you just created on the card-stock paper. The images can be in black and white.

6. Carefully cut around the frame in your image. To cut out the middle of the frame, use the scissor tip to poke a hole through the inside of the frame somewhere and start cutting from there, or make a small cut on the top of the frame and reconstruct it later.

7. Carefully cut out each hieroglyph. Stay as close as possible to the lines. If a hieroglyph consists of a thin line, you can leave a little extra paper around it.

8. Cut the second piece of paper in half lengthwise.

9. Using a glue stick, glue the frame to the center of one of the halves of the second piece of paper.

10. Glue the hieroglyphs inside the frame in the correct order.

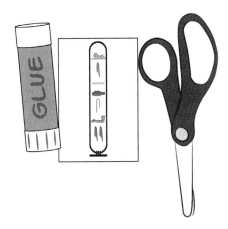

11. Place the second half sheet on top of the first one, covering the frame and hieroglyphs. Align the halves and hold the top one down carefully. Secure it with tape if needed.

12. Hold a sharp colored pencil sideways so that most of the tip is in contact with the paper. Then color over the center area with a firm back-and-forth motion. The images will appear in a darker shade, as shown.

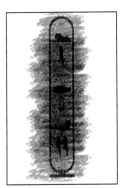

13. After the whole image is colored, cut carefully around the outer edges of the frame.

You may hang the cartouche on your wall. If it's not too long, you can use it as a bookmark for your books on ancient Egypt.

Cartouche of Ptolemy III. It is made out of a glazed ceramic called faience, which was very popular in Egypt. *The Walters Art Museum, Baltimore*

with insufficient guards. The Parthians overpowered the guards and ransacked the wagons. With no equipment or food, the Roman army had no choice but to retreat.

In ancient warfare, a retreat was the very last resort, because it allowed the enemy to strike from behind and caused more losses than a frontal assault. Energized by their advantage, the Parthians pursued the Romans for days, killing them by the thousands. Many more soldiers died of exhaustion, disease, cold, and starvation. Antony, left with about half of his men, struggled to bring the hungry, discouraged, and wounded survivors to safety. At one point he contemplated suicide.

He was physically and emotionally exhausted. The anticipated conquest, which would have given him instant fame and prosperity, had slipped from his hands—and he had only himself to blame.

He had sent letters to Cleopatra asking her to bring money and clothes for his men. He probably wanted comfort more than supplies, which she could have simply sent by messenger—especially since she had just given birth to their third child, Ptolemy Philadelphus.

Plutarch stressed Antony's emotional needs, describing him as "beside himself with distress" when Cleopatra delayed her arrival. According to Plutarch, he tried to drown his apprehension in wine, "although he could not hold out long at table, but in the midst of the drinking would often rise or spring up to look out, until she put into port."

Cleopatra's delay was understandable. It took time to produce enough clothes for thousands of men and organize a fleet of ships to carry both clothing and gold.

At the same time, Octavia, concerned for Antony's well-being, obtained from her brother 2,000 soldiers and 70 ships (what was left of the ships Octavian had borrowed), added a large quantity of her own money and supplies, and started her trip east to meet her husband.

Antony balked. He didn't expect a visit from his wife. He was planning to resume his campaigns, and wives were not supposed to follow their husbands to war. Besides, he was living with Cleopatra during her visit, which must have made the situation awkward, even in a society where men's extramarital affairs were considered normal. He accepted the gifts (even if Octavian was sending one-tenth of what he had promised) but never went to meet his wife.

According to Plutarch, Cleopatra influenced Antony's response, because she went on an all-out attack against her rival. After all, since Antony's marriage to Octavia, Cleopatra hadn't seen him again for over three years and had been left to fend for herself at a time of great political uncertainty. She couldn't let it happen again.

Employing all her charms, she spent more time with Antony and showered him with attention. Knowing both his natural tendency toward compassion and his love of adulation, she lost weight to give the impression that her love had made her ill and made a show of looking ecstatic when he was near and teary eyed when he walked away.

She also found accomplices (among her servants or Antony's men) who could regularly

WRITE AN ANCIENT EGYPTIAN LOVE POEM

Egyptian poets wrote many passionate love poems. Since about 90 percent of the population was illiterate, the authors were usually male scribes, people who read and wrote by profession. Sometimes they wrote poems with a woman's voice, as with the ones included here.

Poetry is distinguished from other forms of writing by different elements. Latin poetry followed special rules for the placement of accented vowels. Some English poetry requires rhymes. Egyptians used techniques like repetition or parallelism (repeating the same idea with different words), which create rhythm and symmetry. In the first poem below, sandwiched between two resolutions ("I shall not leave him" and "I will not listen") you'll find a list of parallel examples of useless attempts to divide the woman from the man she loves.

---

*I shall not leave him even if they beat me
and I have to spend the day in the swamp,
or if they chase me to Syria with clubs,
or to Nubia with palm ribs,
or to the desert with sticks,
or to the coast with reeds.
I will not listen to their plans of giving up
      the man I love.*

In the second poem, three parallel sentences, structured almost the same way, express the same idea ("I want you so much that I can't even finish braiding my hair.")

*My heart thought of my love of you,
When half of my hair was braided.
I came at a run to find you
And neglected my hairdo.
Now if you let me braid my hair
I shall be ready in a moment.*

Write a similar poem, using one of these two techniques.

MATERIALS

➤ Any writing tools (pen and paper, computer, etc.)

1. Choose a person or thing that is dear to your heart.

2. Choose between the two poetry samples above. Write two or three sentences explaining what you want to do with this person or thing, or what they inspire you to do (two bookends, as in the first sample, or three parallel lines, as in the second sample).

3. Add details and practical examples, either between the two statements or after each of the three. For example, highlight the obstacles you are willing to face. Include things you can see, hear, or feel. Each example will stress the same idea but in different ways, painting different mental images.

A sculpture for the tomb of Baker Djehuty and Wife Ahhotep. Thebes, ca. 1500–1450 BC. Egyptians had many statues and portraits of loving couples *The Walters Art Museum, Baltimore*

remind him of her qualities and scold him for his indifference to her pain. After all, they said, Octavia had married him on her brother's request, while Cleopatra, in spite of her high status, had freely chosen to love him.

Apparently Cleopatra's charms had the intended effect, because Antony spent the winter of 35–34 BC in Alexandria, disregarding Octavia and putting aside his military campaigns. There might have been other reasons. He might have still been depressed by his defeat and wanting to retreat to a place where he could put his problems behind him. Or he might have been offended by Octavian's failure to send him all the promised warships and troops.

Unsurprisingly, his decision didn't go over well with Octavian, who advised his sister to move back to Rome into a mansion of her own. Octavia took only half of his advice. She returned to Rome but continued to live in Antony's home, taking care of their two daughters and the boys Antony had with Fulvia, welcoming his friends who were in Rome on business, and continuing to communicate with Octavian on Antony's behalf. In fact, she told her brother to ignore Antony's mistreatment of her for the sake of unity.

By this time, however, Octavian didn't seem interested in unity. The triumvirate had been founded on a temporary need rather than a common vision. Lepidus had been expelled for making a bad political move, and the remaining triumvirs had split the empire neatly between them. The division of lands allowed them to act independently. It also seemed to match their separate dreams and personalities. Octavian preferred to stay in Rome and improve matters in the city, while Antony loved the Greek lifestyle and wanted to expand the empire.

An Unusual Celebration

In the spring of 34 BC, Antony got minor revenge on his enemies by defeating King Artavasdes of Armenia, who had allied with the Parthians in the previous war. While small, it was his first victory since Philippi and allowed him to strengthen the Roman borders in the east. He also cemented an alliance with the king of Media (also named Artavasdes) by arranging a marriage between the king's daughter and his son with Cleopatra, Alexander Helios, to take place as soon as the children came of age.

To celebrate these successes, he returned to Alexandria in a triumphal chariot, dragging behind him the conquered Armenian king as well as the king's wife and sons—all bound with silver or gold chains to emphasize their importance. The celebration was much grander than the victory called for, but Antony needed to boost his spirits with a splendid display.

Once again, he dressed as Dionysus—god of victory as well as of wine—wearing a crown of ivy and a golden robe and holding the god's sacred wand. After the crushing defeat in Parthia, he was gaining his confidence back.

Cleopatra rose to the occasion, decking out the city in typical Ptolemaic splendor, filling Alexandria with colorful banners, music, and dance.

MAKE EGYPTIAN CASTANETS

During festivals, Egyptians used many types of musical instruments, including flutes, double pipes, harps, drums, rattles, tambourines, and castanets. You can make a simple pair of castanets with a few materials you may have at home.

MATERIALS

- Ruler or measuring tape
- Scissors
- Any thin recycled cardboard (for example, an empty cardboard box)
- Paintbrush and paint, markers, and/or stickers
- Hole puncher
- 4 solid brass fasteners, 2 inches long

1. Measure the length of your middle finger from the tip to the bottom (where it meets your palm). Multiply that number by two.

2. Using scissors, cut two rectangular pieces of cardboard. The rectangles should be your double finger measurement long and 2 inches wide.

3. Using paint, markers, and/or stickers, color and decorate one side of each piece as you like. Let any paint or marker dry completely before moving on to the next step.

4. Once the cardboard is dry, fold each piece of cardboard in half, bringing the two undecorated sides together so that the decorated side is on the outside.

5. Using a hole puncher, make a center hole ½ inch from each short end of both pieces of cardboard. If you don't have a hole puncher, you can carefully poke the holes using the scissor tip.

6. Insert a 2-inch brass fastener in each hole so that the head of the fastener is on the undecorated side of the cardboard.

7. Open each fastener and bend the ends to form a ring. For each piece of cardboard, make sure one of its rings is large enough for your thumb and the other for your middle finger.

8. Hold one piece of cardboard in each hand, with the crease facing your palm, and insert your thumb in the bigger ring and your middle finger in the smaller ring.

9. Open and close your hands so that the fastener heads bang against each other. Make music!

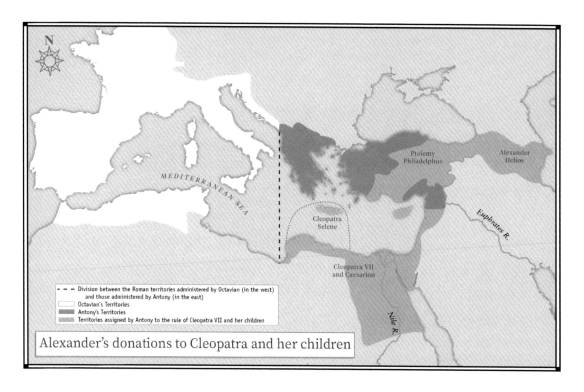

Alexander's donations to Cleopatra and her children

uniquely granted by the Roman Senate and held solely in Rome, where it ended with a sacrifice to Jupiter, the king of Roman gods, not with a tribute to a foreign queen!

The outrage had barely begun to spread when, a few days later, Antony and Cleopatra held another grand ceremony, this time in the Alexandrian gymnasium, where they sat on two golden thrones set on a silver platform. Antony was once again dressed as Dionysus, while Cleopatra wore the tight black tunic typical of Isis. In front of them sat Cleopatra's children, including Caesarion, each clothed in the royal robes characteristic of the countries they were to oversee.

Then Antony began his official declaration in Greek. Cleopatra and 13-year-old Caesarion were to rule Egypt, Cyprus, Libya, and central Syria. Six-year-old Alexander Helios was proclaimed king of Armenia, Media, and Parthia, while his twin sister, Cleopatra Selene, was given rule of Cyrenaica and Crete. Two-year-old Ptolemy received Phoenicia, Cilicia, and the rest of Syria.

Cleopatra was hailed as "Queen of Kings and her Sons who are Kings" and Caesarion "King of Kings." The fact that she sat above her children—Caesarion included—confirmed that she was still superior to them.

This division of property promised some security. She had learned from history that sibling rivalry was a serious threat in a royal family. Even if Caesarion was the heir to the throne, in time her other children might look for opportunities to take over, and making them rulers over different parts of her territories was a possible remedy.

She sat on a golden throne on top of a silver-plated platform, waiting for Antony and a procession of acclaiming Roman crowds. Though supportive of Antony's victory over the king, the crowds did not come to Cleopatra's defense when Artavasdes and his nobles stubbornly refused to bow to the queen.

It was an unprecedented humiliation for Cleopatra and her subjects. Surprisingly, the prisoners were not executed for their disrespect but were simply held captive. Antony might have decided on this leniency, as he, like Caesar, was known for showing mercy toward his enemies.

Octavian reacted with shock. Regardless of Antony's intentions, the ceremony appeared too similar to a Roman triumph—a celebration

Writing in the early 20th century, Greek poet Constantine P. Cavafy described this celebration as he imagined it:

An Alexandrian crowd collected
to see the sons of Cleopatra,
Caesarion and his little brothers
Alexander and Ptolemy, who for the first
time were brought to the Gymnasium,
there to be crowned as kings
amidst a splendid display of troops.

It was a spectacular celebration, but Cavafy, who was also a historian, knew that few people were fooled.

And the Alexandrians ran to see the show
and grew enthusiastic, and applauded
in Greek, in Egyptian, and some in Hebrew,
bewitched with the beautiful spectacle,
though they knew perfectly well how worthless,
what empty words, were these king-makings.

Was Cavafy correct? Were these just empty words? Octavian thought so. Antony didn't have the power to give a foreign ruler any Roman territory he wished—territories that Roman soldiers had risked their lives to conquer. Once again rumors spread that Antony and Cleopatra were aiming at the eventual overthrow of the Roman government.

In reality, the ceremony was a confirmation of the territories assigned to Cleopatra three years earlier, as well as a way to impress on the spectacle-hungry Alexandrians the power of the royal family as Rome's client rulers. Antony included the children as a sign of a bright future, fully aware that they were too young to rule and that some territories, like Parthia, had not yet been conquered.

In Rome his motives didn't seem to matter. In spite of his expressions of loyalty for his country, many Romans began to doubt it. The distance allowed for much gossip, and the exotic flavor of Egypt inspired fanciful exaggerations. The Roman poet Horace, for example, described Antony as a slave of the queen, so unmanly that, fearing insect bites, he shielded himself with mosquito nets during a military parade. A friend of Octavian spread word that, as a payment of a lost bet, Antony had to wash Cleopatra's feet at a crowded banquet—a very humiliating act for a Roman general. He added that Antony had taken 20,000 scrolls from the renowned Library of Pergamum, in today's Turkey, to give to Cleopatra for the Library of Alexandria.

The number is so far-fetched that the story is generally considered false, along with other tales of Antony's infatuation with Cleopatra—an infatuation that allegedly compelled him to interrupt important court hearings to read her love notes or to abandon meetings altogether if she was passing by on her litter. In every case, the message was the same: such a spellbound man could no longer act in Rome's best interests.

The Sharers of Death

Why have you changed? —Antony to Octavian

One person's misfortune can be another's opportunity, and Octavian was quick to capitalize on Antony's poor reputation. He just added fuel to the fire, and the fuel was easy to find. Antony's impulsive and pleasure-seeking lifestyle had led him to make many objectionable choices in his life.

"Why have you changed?" Antony wrote back in frustration. There had been better times for the two men when they fought for a common cause and shared some fun on the side. If Cleopatra was the reason for Octavian's turnabout, Antony told him in coarse and explicit language to mind his own business. Yes, Antony had been with Cleopatra nine years, but he saw nothing wrong with

An artist's view of the Battle of Actium, with ships burning. *Heritage History, www.heritage-history.com*

that. In fact, he questioned Octavian's faithfulness to his wife, Livia, as if to say, "Doesn't everyone do it?"

In the eyes of Romans, the comparison didn't hold. Yes, most influential men in Rome had extramarital affairs, and yes, Octavian had been no exception. Still, from a purely political point of view, the public was willing to let those things go on account of Octavian's young age (he was only 30), his loyalty to Rome, and the fact that his romantic escapades had been short lived and contained within the city limits. Antony, by contrast, was a 50-year-old man who had maintained

Marcus Vipsanius Agrippa.
Erich Lessing / Art Resource, NY

a long-term relationship with a foreign queen in apparent disregard for his country's welfare.

The Inevitable Conflict

The triumvirs' war of words continued to mount as they kept finding new accusations to fling at each other. It was soon obvious that it was much more than a petty argument. Both men were ultimately eager for power.

A civil war seemed inevitable, but the outcome was not predictable. On the one hand, Antony, with longer military experience and the eastern provinces at his disposal, seemed stronger. Octavian, on the other hand, had the support of the majority of Rome's population and a trump card to play: Marcus Vipsanius Agrippa, a clever general and architect who had become Octavian's close friend and son-in-law and had contributed to some major Roman victories.

In the summer of 33 BC, Antony's legions assembled in the region of the Euphrates River, as if they were preparing for a new strike on Parthia. Instead of moving east, however, he ordered them to march west, toward Greece. Since there was no threat in that region, it might have been a provocation aimed at Octavian. To keep the support of the Roman people, who were tired of civil wars and wary of dictators, the triumvirs had to play their cards right, each provoking the other to attack first.

Cleopatra and Antony prepared for war in the winter, sailing from Alexandria with 200 Egyptian ships and heading for Athens with the intention of gathering more warships, troops, and supplies from their eastern colonies. Besides ships and sailors, Cleopatra had provided 20,000 talents—twice the amount her father had once given Aulus Gabinius. Her fate and the fate of her country were now more than ever tied to Antony.

A Convenient Enemy

A few months later, Antony divorced Octavia, cutting his last ties with her brother. Divorcing wives who were no longer convenient was not unusual among Roman leaders. In this case, however, the rejection of the beloved Octavia provoked great indignation in Rome, further damaging Antony's reputation. Even in Athens, people reacted angrily, judging by graffiti on one of Antony's statues that read (half in Greek and half in Latin), "Octavia and Athena [patron goddess of Athens] to Antony: Pack up your things and go!"

To make things worse, in the summer of the same year, a former friend of Antony revealed to Octavian the whereabouts of Antony's last will. Antony kept it in the Temple of Vesta, the virgin Roman goddess of home and family. Unconcerned about his disrespect for a sacred place, Octavian stormed into the temple and seized the document from the high priestess's hands.

Next he read the will's shocking contents publicly in the Forum: Antony had left an inheritance to all his children with Cleopatra and had asked to be buried next to her in Alexandria. The will simply confirmed what many suspected was Antony's attitude toward the queen and their children. He certainly knew that leaving an inheritance to non-citizens was illegal in Rome, but he might have been planning to gain citizenship for his children.

Whatever the case, the will served Octavian's purpose, creating national fury. It was the piece of propaganda he needed. At the end of the summer, after rumors had swirled for some time, he called for a traditional war ceremony in the Temple of Bellona (goddess of war) on the Campus Martius (Field of Mars, the main war-god of Rome). There, priests dipped a spear in the blood of a sacrificial animal and threw the spear onto a designated patch of grass, fighting against an invisible foreign enemy, officially declaring war on Cleopatra and Cleopatra alone—with no mention of Antony. Cleopatra was the enemy who had subjugated Antony and, according to rumors, was intent on ruling over Rome and making Alexandria the official capital of her empire.

Suddenly Roman citizens who had long been discouraged and divided found a reason to enthusiastically unite on behalf of their country and the republic. Cleopatra inspired both outrage and fear. "All Italy," Octavian boasted later, "swore allegiance to me voluntarily, and demanded me as leader of the war . . . ; the provinces of Gaul, Spain, Africa, Sicily, and Sardinia swore the same allegiance."

An Uncomfortable Presence

If Antony's supporters knew that Cleopatra was not the enemy, they still found her presence awkward during the preparations for war: a distraction to Antony and a detriment to his cause. Some respected her for Antony's sake, while others became more outspoken against her. Even one of Antony's most faithful advocates refused to address her with an honorific title and simply called her by her first name.

Who was she anyhow? A queen? Then how was she different from any other client rulers who had come to help Antony? Why was she allowed to be by his side day and night, giving him advice?

A papyrus granting an enormous tax break to Publius Canidius. At the bottom is the Greek word ginesthoi, "let it be so," written in a different hand on February 23, 33 BC. Some scholars believe Cleopatra wrote it. If so, it would be the only existing example of her handwriting. *bpk Bildagentur / Aegyptisches Museum, Staatliche Museen, Berlin, Germany / Margarete Buesing / Art Resource, NY*

Their romantic bond provided no excuse. Antony knew quite well that it was not proper to bring a wife to combat, much less to blatantly parade a mistress—especially a foreign one!

The situation came to a head when a senator named Geminius arrived in Greece from Rome. According to Plutarch, Cleopatra was immediately suspicious, thinking he had come to reunite Antony with Octavia. To be safe, she seated him at a far distance from Antony at meals and made him the butt of jokes and derision. Geminius took it in silence.

It was only at the end of a banquet that someone finally asked him why he was there. He hesitated (he would have preferred to wait until everyone was sober) but finally revealed he had come with a message: if Antony wanted success, he had to send Cleopatra back to Egypt.

This time Cleopatra didn't have to say or do anything. To her delight, Antony flew into a rage and sent Geminius packing instead of her.

There is record of only one man in favor of the queen's presence, but his motives have been questioned. This man was Publius Canidius Crassus, one of Antony's most loyal generals, who couldn't "see how Cleopatra was inferior in intelligence to anyone of the princes who took part in the expedition." She had governed a large kingdom by herself, had contributed greatly to Antony's battles, and, by living with him, had expanded her knowledge of politics and war.

Canidius's words sound rational and true. But Cleopatra had given him enormous tax breaks, allowing him to export huge quantities of wheat from Egypt and import large quantities of wine without paying taxes on either, plus granting him exemption from any tax on his Egyptian properties (a grant Egyptologist Toby Wilkinson has described as "one of the biggest and boldest" political bribes in history). According to Plutarch, she had bribed Canidius again in this case in order to gain his backing.

Despite his people's prevailing attitudes about Cleopatra, Antony's reaction proves that her presence was essential to him. He had apparently become dependent on her emotional support.

The Battle of Actium

By the end of summer, Antony's forces were finally stationed in a few harbors on the western coast of Greece, with their headquarters in Patrae, a small town on the Gulf of Corinth. He had gathered 500 warships and 300 merchant ships (including Cleopatra's). His infantry amounted to 100,000 men, and his cavalry to 12,000. Counting Cleopatra, he had seven subject rulers by his side, while five more had sent him soldiers and supplies.

Octavian's preparations, by contrast, were lagging. His final count was 250 warships, 80,000 infantry, and about 12,000 cavalry. If Antony had launched a surprise attack on Italy at that time, he might have triumphed. With Cleopatra by his side, however, it would have looked like a foreign invasion, with Antony fighting against his own country for the love of the queen. He might have won a military battle, but the whole of Italy might have risen against him.

He decided to wait, clearly aware that waiting for an enemy attack was risky. That's what Pompey, Brutus, and Cassius had done, and they had all lost.

War officially broke out in the spring of 31 BC. Antony placed his troops on the **promontory** of Actium, off the western coast of Greece. He planned to use the Actium plain for the battle while keeping two nearby ports as supply lines.

Octavian's star general Agrippa attacked first—from the south, where Antony had least expected it and had placed only an isolated outpost. For

A silver coin Antony issued before the Battle of Actium to pay his soldiers. On one side is a warship, symbolizing the strength of his fleet (largely thanks to Cleopatra's contribution). On the back is an eagle between two legionary standards. *Classical Numismatic Group, Inc., www.cngcoins.com*

The Gulf of Actium. *Dan Diffendale, Flickr*

Agrippa, it meant a longer sailing time, with the danger of running out of supplies or being caught in a storm, but it was worth it, allowing him to gain a base in the south early in the battle. From there, he continued to conquer small cities on the coast, threatening Antony's supply lines. Taking advantage of Antony's surprise, Octavian moved his troops to the north virtually unopposed. Antony was blocked on both sides.

Initially Antony and Cleopatra kept their composure, confident in Antony's military abilities and the strength of their armies. Soon, however, they were forced to face the grim reality: With limited supplies, Antony's men became weaker and susceptible to disease, especially in the malaria-ridden swamp where they had set up camp. Many died.

The survivors started to doubt their reasons for fighting. Many fled the scene. Some, including some of Antony's client kings, **defected**, or switched sides, to Octavian. Some strange and unconfirmed stories include that of a failed plan by Octavian's men to kidnap Antony and of a fake attempt by Cleopatra to poison her lover. This second story is told by Pliny, who explained how Antony had become so fearful and distrusting of others (including Cleopatra) that he had a servant taste all his food to make sure it was not poisoned. Playing on his fears, Cleopatra took a ring of flowers, called a garland, that had been prepared for wearing at a meal (a widespread custom in many ancient countries, including Egypt), secretly wet the flowers' tips with poison, then placed it on his head.

At one point during the dinner, she proposed that they "drink" their garlands—a common tradition of crushing the flowers and dropping them in wine. Before unsuspecting Antony's lips could touch his flower-wine mixture, she stopped him and revealed her scheme. "Look, Mark Antony," she said, "I am the one you are trying to prevent with your new preoccupation for tasters! If I could live without you, this is how much I lack the opportunity [to do it]." In reality, she couldn't live without him. Her destiny was tied to his.

True or false, the story highlights Antony's agitation. He knew he couldn't stay on the defensive. Canidius, who commanded Antony's land troops, suggested abandoning the fleet and marching north to Macedonia, where they could fight in better conditions. After all, Antony's success had always been in land battles, and he had many experienced foot soldiers at his disposal.

The suggestion was dismissed. According to Plutarch, Cleopatra was not willing to abandon her ships and treasures (too bulky to be carried over land) and advised Antony to return to Egypt, where they could regroup. Dio wrote that she had been terrified by a series of bad omens (for example, swallows nesting on her ship and around her tent, milk and blood dripping together from beeswax, and statues of herself and Antony hurled down by lightning) and had "filled Antony with fears."

Any escape had to be carefully executed, because an open retreat would have further discouraged the already disheartened and weak troops and would have emboldened the enemy to launch a fiercer attack. Finally Antony and Cleopatra agreed to fake a naval battle and then break through the enemy lines.

MAKE A GARLAND

Garlands of flowers were very common in the ancient world. They were used to decorate the heads of the dead before burial, and they were also worn during parties. Make a garland, wear it, and celebrate!

MATERIALS

- Braided headband (or yarn to make one)
- Scissors
- 5 or more flowers (depending on the size), fresh or silk
- Hair clips (optional, only if you use silk flowers and don't want to cut the stems)

1. If you need to make your own headband, wrap a length of yarn around your head like a crown, starting at the middle of your forehead, and mark this measurement. Cut the yarn about three inches longer than this measurement, then cut two more pieces of yarn the same length. Knot the three pieces of yarn together at one end, braid the pieces, and make a knot at the opposite end. Make sure it fits around your head, then tie both ends together to create a ring.

2. Cut the stems from five or more flowers so they are 1 inch long.

3. Open one link of the braid and insert a flower stem.

4. Turn the braid around and insert the stem into the next link to hold the flower in place.

5. Repeat steps 3 and 4 for the rest of the flowers.

6. Wear the garland on your head like a crown.

Tip: If you are using silk flowers and don't want to cut off so much of the stems (in case you want to place them in a vase later), you can insert the flowers without their stems instead. Simply snap each flower off its stem and set the stem aside. You can reattach them later if you choose. Insert the flowers in the braid and hold them in place with hair clips.

While waiting for suitable weather, they decreased the number of their ships to match the reduced number of soldiers, burning the rest to prevent the Romans from increasing their naval strength by seizing the abandoned ships. Cleopatra was left with 60 ships. Some land soldiers were sent to the naval battle, and the rest were assigned to Canidius, who had the duty of marching them to safety.

The battle started on September 2. Antony took command of the center fleet, with Cleopatra and her fleet behind him. In those days, naval battles were very similar to those fought on land, with ships from each side lined up facing each other, waiting for the signal to attack. Each enemy ship was like a fortress to be overtaken, either by ramming it full force with one's own ship or getting close enough to board it and continuing the battle on deck. Soldiers could also destroy ships by launching fiery darts into them, but this was a last resort, because it ruined the valuable cargo on board, cargo they hoped to get for themselves.

Some of Antony's sailors wondered why their ships carried sails—something unusual for warships at battle. Antony explained the sails were necessary in case they decided to chase an enemy ship. In reality, he planned to raise them as soon as his ships had a clear passageway and use the strength of the wind to flee toward Egypt.

The fleets waited patiently in the uncomfortable stillness until the strong north-northwest wind, which usually picked up around noon, started to blow behind them. Antony gave the signal to proceed.

Initially the strike seemed successful, as both Agrippa's and Octavian's fleets began to retreat. In reality, the retreat was a tactical move. Agrippa wanted to force Antony's and Cleopatra's boats to come farther out to sea, where he could surround them. As soon as Agrippa had enough room to execute his plan, he turned around and attacked.

Ramming wasn't effective against the large ships employed in this war, so Agrippa opted for an ingenious weapon of his own invention called a *harpax*: a grappling hook attached to a rope and shot from a catapult. When shot, the *harpax* could hook the side of an enemy ship, and soldiers could use the rope to pull the ship closer. Agrippa wrestled to find the right position as Antony's ships moved around to avoid him. Amid that uneasy dance, a large gap opened up, and Cleopatra's squad was quick to move through it, hoisting its sails. As soon as the sails caught the wind, the ship progressed too fast to be chased by the enemy's sail-less ships.

Antony saw her. Moving by rowboat from his large ship to a smaller vessel prepared for the flight, he hoisted the sail and followed his lover. About seventy of his ships trailed behind, while the others stayed back and continued the fight. Eventually some that stayed behind were sunk or burned, and some surrendered. Discouraged, weary, and short of supplies, Antony's army admitted defeat, except for Canidius, who fled secretly at night and caught up with Antony.

Antony had lost more than the war—he had lost his honor and reputation as a Roman general by putting his life before that of his men. Fleeing

A temple to Poseidon, Greek god of the sea, at Cape Tainaron.
Mike With, Flickr

and leaving part of his army to fend for itself was completely contrary to the concept of *virtus* (loosely translated, "courage and correctness") that was embedded in Roman culture. And to many, his following Cleopatra seemed to confirm that he had become the queen's pawn.

An Unfortunate Plan

From her ship Cleopatra sent Antony a signal, inviting him to join her. By rowboat, he moved sheepishly to her ship, where, according to Plutarch, he sat alone at the prow "in silence, holding his head in both hands." Only a few days later, when they landed at the southernmost point of mainland Greece (today's Cape Tainaron), Cleopatra's closest maidservants persuaded Antony to spend the day with the queen. There, for the first time after the war, the lovers talked and ate together, as they continued to do for the rest of the journey. A while later, more ships arrived from Actium, bringing a ray of encouragement.

After this meeting, the two lovers separated again. Cleopatra went back to her capital, while Antony tried to put together another army—a very bleak prospect. His main hopes rested on four legions he had left in Cyrenaica, but he soon received news that they had defected to Octavian. The report was so heartbreaking that Antony's friends had to forcibly stop him from committing suicide.

Cleopatra was not about to give up. After all, she had survived 39 years of power struggles, violence, threats, betrayals, exile, and national crises. Like many of Antony's client kings, she entertained thoughts of surrendering to Octavian. The move would have required intense negotiations, however, because she was not ready to lose either her country or her honor.

The first thing to do was rush to Alexandria before news of her and Antony's defeat could reach the city. Defeat meant weakness, and as she had learned from her family history, a weak ruler was often overthrown or killed. Once there, she entered as though she were a victor, sailing into the Great Harbor with garlands on her prows and joyous songs being played on her decks.

After a celebratory ride to her palace, she engineered her next move: the execution of any man who could take advantage of her loss. As a side benefit, she could confiscate their properties and replenish some of the goods she had lost in the war. To remedy the rest of her losses, she increased taxes and took gold and other valuable objects from Egypt's temples.

The funds came in handy for a new plan of escape: she ordered the construction of new ships near the Red Sea and the transportation of her existing ships there via the Canal of the Pharaohs, an overland channel that connected the Nile to the Gulf of Suez. It was a forerunner of the Suez Canal but followed a different course.

These ships could transport Cleopatra, her children, and probably Antony to a safe land (maybe India) where they could live in exile. After all, she knew from experience that times of exile can be productive.

The plan failed miserably, however, when the first of her ships to arrive at the Red Sea were attacked and burned by the king of Nabataea, who was hoping to gain Octavian's favor. With her plans to flee east defeated and any route to the west blocked by Roman armies, Cleopatra was stuck.

Dying Hopes

Antony arrived in Alexandria visibly depressed. Instead of moving in with Cleopatra, he stayed in a new structure built on an isolated pier, where he nursed his sorrow. Only after much persuasion was the queen able to bring him back to her palace, where she surrounded him with the same comfort and luxury that had cheered him many times before. According to Plutarch, she involved the whole city in "the enjoyment of suppers and drinking-bouts and distributions of gifts."

Special festivities were held for Caesarion and Antyllus (Antony's first son with Fulvia), who came of age around that time. Cleopatra observed Caesarion's 16th birthday with a splendid Greek-style ceremony that officially added him to the list of young Alexandrian male citizens. Antyllus, who had been staying in Alexandria with his father, was turning 14 and, according to Roman customs, was able to wear his very first toga virilis (manly toga)—a sign of manhood and full participation in the life of Roman citizens. As typical in these cases, the commemorations lasted for days and included offerings to the gods and an abundance of food. In those dark days, the festivities provided people with a distraction from the harsh reality of war and a message of hope: if anything happened to their parents, these boys were now ready to lead.

Overall, Antony and Cleopatra knew their future was bleak. Octavian had proved himself determined to eliminate Antony, and Cleopatra—whom Octavian had used as a reason for the civil war—could not expect much mercy. She started to experiment with poisons, testing them on condemned prisoners to see which produced the quickest and least painful end. Disbanding their society of fun-loving Inimitables, the two lovers formed a new group—equally luxurious and extravagant—with an ominous name: the Sharers of Death.

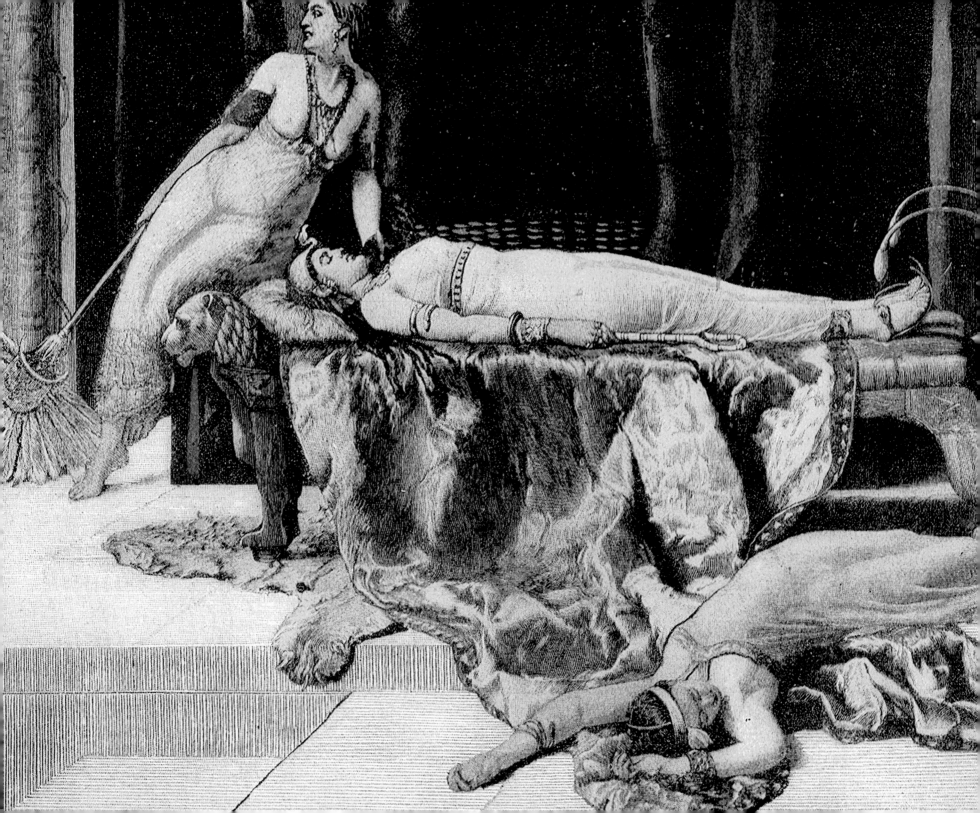

8

The End of an Era

Bid farewell to her, to Alexandria who is departing. —Cavafy

While resigning themselves to the idea of death, Antony and Cleopatra continued to grasp at any prospect of life. They both sent a constant stream of letters to Octavian, pleading for mercy. Antony played on his long-standing friendship with the Roman conqueror and offered to retire from public life and move to Greece if Octavian didn't want him in Egypt. Cleopatra assured Octavian of her loyalty to Rome. She probably added generous gifts and promised to send more if he would only allow her or her children to rule over at least parts of their kingdom.

Octavian never replied to Antony, not even when Antyllus was sent to Rome with gifts. To Cleopatra, Octavian offered mercy in exchange for Antony's

Ruins of the ancient city of Pelusium, located on what was once the eastern-most mouth of the Nile River. Pelusium was the main eastern frontier fortress and a station on the trade route to the Red Sea. *Gunter Hartnagel, Flickr*

A Last Resistance

Octavian didn't rush to Egypt. He had other important matters at hand and was sure that Egypt was already in his grasp. Finally, in the summer of 30 BC, he sent armies to attack from two directions: from Syria in the east and from Cyrenaica in the west. Antony tried to muster troops in a desperate defense of the western front, but his efforts ended in failure. The fortified city of Pelusium, a bastion of Egyptian defense, surrendered quickly, apparently without a fight. Dio attributed the submission to Cleopatra, who had given orders for the city to yield to Octavian. Plutarch agreed that there were rumors to that effect, adding that she allowed Antony to punish the commander of her troops at Pelusium by executing both his wife and children. If she had in fact ordered the surrender, the punishment would have been a way to cover up her actions.

In spite of this loss, Antony caught up with Octavian's leading troops, or **vanguard**, and was able to stop them from entering the city. Lifted by the rush of victory, he entered Alexandria and, before even taking off his armor, ran to hug Cleopatra, introducing his bravest soldier to her. Dutifully, she rewarded the soldier with a golden helmet and breastplate. The man accepted but, the same night, left Antony's army to defect to Octavian.

Antony sent a message to Octavian, challenging him to single combat. Octavian declined, mockingly reminding his old companion that there were many ways to die. Antony himself must not have held high hopes, because that night,

life or his banishment from Egypt. Of course, Antony was not included in these communications, but the stream of messengers from Rome to Cleopatra was enough to raise his suspicions, to the point that Antony ordered the flogging of the messenger who spent the most time in private discussions with the queen.

Cleopatra went out of her way to reassure her lover. Understating her own 39th birthday party, she prepared an elaborate celebration for Antony, who turned 53 on January 14. In fact, his festivities were so extravagant that many of the guests "came poor and went away rich," according to Plutarch. Antony didn't know that Cleopatra had already sent Octavian her golden scepter, crown, and royal throne in a sign of utter submission.

when the Sharers of Death dined together, he told his servants to serve generous portions: no one knew what the next day might bring. They might be serving a new master. To his clearly distressed friends, he confessed he just wanted to die an honorable death.

Outside the palace, the Alexandrians shared similar feelings of fear and despair. Some heard music, songs, and shouting—the same sounds people made during festivals to Dionysus. This went along with the Greco-Roman belief that the gods associated with a city would leave just before a disaster. In this case, the departing god was Dionysus, with whom Antony had associated himself all his life.

Commenting on this episode, Cavafy wrote:

When at the hour of midnight
an invisible choir is suddenly heard passing
with exquisite music, with voices—
Do not lament your fortune that at last subsides,
your life's work that has failed, your schemes that
    have proved illusions.
But like a man prepared, like a brave man,
bid farewell to her, to Alexandria who is departing.

The Inevitable Defeat

Any hope Antony may have harbored vanished the next day when his plans went awry. He had decided to start with a naval attack on Octavian's fleet, following it with an assault on land, but what followed left him speechless. After approaching the enemy as planned, all his warships together raised their oars out of the water in surrender to Octavian, joined the enemy forces, and turned against the city. His cavalry followed suit, defecting en masse. He was left only with his infantry, which was easily defeated.

Shaken and crushed, he retired to the city, shouting that Cleopatra had betrayed him—a cruel reward, he thought, since the war had been waged for her sake. In the meantime, she had moved with her two closest maidservants, Charmion and Iras, into a stately **mausoleum** prepared for her burial. There, she had amassed all her royal treasures, surrounding them with flammable material—maybe as a threat to Octavian: if he attacked her, she would destroy her fortune, which he obviously needed.

She had also taken some supplies and bolted the door so that it could not be opened from the outside. The mausoleum had two floors. The only openings were the door below and one or more windows above.

According to the early sources she instructed a messenger to bring Antony news of her death. At that point, Antony's anger turned to grief. Back in his room, he asked a servant to pierce a sword through his chest. As frequent as suicide was in those days, methods seen as honorable ways to escape humiliation weren't easy to perform. Many times something went wrong, leaving the victim to suffer for days. For this reason, Antony had chosen a trusted servant who had practiced the moves carefully. Surprisingly, this servant raised the sword to his own breast, stabbing himself instead of his master.

Left by himself, Antony tried to do the same but missed his heart and pierced his stomach. Gripped with pain and weakness, he fainted briefly on a couch. When he regained consciousness, he cried out to others to please put an end to his life, but no one answered. Just then, he received news that Cleopatra was alive. Dio said she heard Antony's cries and went to her window, where someone saw her. Antony ordered his men to take him to her.

Did Cleopatra engineer the military defection, or was it just Antony's assumption? Did she send a messenger to tell him she was dead, or was it just a rumor? Both Plutarch and Dio suggest she did, and the idea is not unlikely. After all, Cleopatra knew Antony had no hope of winning. Her actions might have been intended to both hurry along an unavoidable end and win Octavian's favor.

If this was the case, any such practical thoughts must have faded when she saw from her window the bleeding body of her lover. Still unwilling to open the door for fear of being caught, she found a way to lift him up to one of the windows through a system of pulleys—the same that were used to lift stone blocks onto a building. Plutarch paints a pitiful image: "Smeared with blood and struggling with death he was drawn up, stretching out his hands to her even as he dangled in the air."

As soon as he was inside, Cleopatra gave in to extreme expressions of mourning (such as were common in Mediterranean countries): tearing her clothes, beating and scratching her breasts, and smearing his blood on her face. She called him "master, husband, and imperator." She only stopped when Antony asked for a drink of wine, either to quench his thirst or to numb his pain.

He died soon after. Before dying, he gave her one last recommendation: find reliable men to help her. Of Octavian's men, he suggested a friend named Gaius Proculeius. This might have been a sign of poor judgment or excessive trust on Antony's part, because Proculeius was completely on Octavian's side and had his own interests in mind.

Wretched Cleopatra

In the meantime, one of Antony's bodyguards brought his leader's bloodstained sword to Octavian, who is said to have retired to his tent to cry.

An artist's representation of Antony's death in Cleopatra's arms (1760, by Pompeo Batoni). *Scala / White Images / Art Resource, NY*

It's hard to know whether they were tears of sincere sorrow. He had certainly anticipated Antony's death. Of course, the pair had at one point been allies and friends.

Octavian soon marched his troops into the city, following the wide Canopic Way boulevard to the gymnasium. There, he reassured the fearful Alexandrians that he would treat them fairly, in honor of Alexander the Great, of their beautiful and spacious city, and of his own tutor Areius, who had studied at the Alexandrian Museum and had accompanied him on this trip.

Since Antony had taken his own life, Octavian was spared the difficult task of executing or punishing a man the Alexandrians—normally critical of their rulers—had actually come to love. To prove his own fairness, he read them a series of letters that showed how much wisdom and patience he had shown in spite of Antony's rude and arrogant remarks. Of course, the letters were handpicked to serve that purpose, but generally speaking, Antony was known to be impulsive and ready to speak his mind, while Octavian was cautious with his words.

After this meeting, Octavian quickly moved on to the next phase of his conquest: getting Cleopatra out of the mausoleum—a task he assigned to Proculeius. Cleopatra remembered that name. Trusting Antony's recommendation, she went downstairs to talk with this messenger through the bolted door. Proculeius told her to be optimistic and trust Octavian.

He was really there to scout the situation. He returned later with a commander named Cornelius Gallus, who was also a highly literate poet. Once again Cleopatra went to the door, where Gallus managed to keep her attention while Proculeius placed a high ladder under a window and climbed into the building with two other men.

As the three descended to the lower floor, one of Cleopatra's maids saw them and cried, with an expression typical of Greek tragedies, "Wretched Cleopatra, you are taken alive!" The queen turned around, instinctively putting a hand to the dagger she had hidden inside her clothes, but Proculeius stopped her by running forward and blocking her with both hands. In an attempt to calm her down, he explained that she was doing wrong both to herself and to Octavian, depriving him of a chance to show his great kindness. After all, he said, Octavian was "the gentlest of commanders."

Those words must have reminded Cleopatra of the messenger who, almost ten years earlier, had encouraged her to meet at Tarsus "the most agreeable and humane of commanders"—in that case Antony. Could Proculeius be right? This thought and Antony's recommendation might have encouraged her to yield to the capture and the search for weapons.

A Last Attempt

Cleopatra and her maids were allowed to stay in the mausoleum for a while to oversee Antony's **embalming**. Then they were brought to her palace, where they were kept under the strict supervision of a freed Roman slave. Out of respect for Antony's wishes, Octavian allowed Cleopatra to organize his funeral and burial and to attend it under guard. When she did, she yielded once again to loud and violent expressions of mourning, so much that some of her scratches later became infected. Feverish, she lost the desire to eat but strengthened herself when she heard that Octavian wanted to see her. He was her last hope.

Given her history of first encounters with Roman generals, she must have planned the meeting carefully to impress Octavian—this time not with her intelligence (as she had done with Caesar) or with her riches (as she had done with Antony) but with her loyalty and submission.

Dio and Plutarch described her appearance very differently. According to Plutarch, she wore only a simple tunic and lay on a humble mat, her eyes lifeless and hair messy, whereas Dio wrote that she dressed to perfection and reclined on a golden couch.

In both stories, she tried to move Octavian to compassion, whether by opening her tunic just enough to show her scratched-up chest or by surrounding herself with pictures and busts of Caesar, clutching his letters to her bosom and often gently kissing them. Plutarch said that she shifted all the blame on Antony, stating in a trembling voice that she was forced to obey him. When Octavian refuted all her excuses, she simply begged for pity.

Both historians also included a discussion of financial matters. According to Plutarch, a royal attendant contradicted the queen's list of properties, affirming she had more valuables than she had reported to Octavian, and the queen grabbed him by the hair and slapped him repeatedly.

She then justified herself by saying she had not counted some jewels, but it was only because she had intended to donate them to Octavian's wife and sister, hoping for their help in return.

Octavian didn't say much. In fact, he tried not to look at her directly. According to both historians, he was glad that Cleopatra begged for her life, because his goal was to take her to Rome alive as a spoil of war. Since no female prisoner had ever been executed in Rome, it's safe to assume she would have been given a comfortable place to retire in luxury, as her sister Arsinoe had in Ephesus, before being assassinated. She certainly wouldn't have been allowed to rule. After all, she had been the ultimate enemy in his rallying cry for war.

The End of a Dream

This was far from what Cleopatra was hoping. How could the New Isis, the proud Queen of the Two Lands, be dragged through the streets of Rome in chains? She couldn't, explained Horace. She refused, "not a humble woman, to be led as a private citizen in an arrogant triumph."

If she had nursed any hopes of changing Octavian's mind, they were soon crushed when one of his officers warned her that his general was planning to take her and her children to Rome three days later.

With renewed urgency, she asked for permission to visit Antony's body, which was laid out in her mausoleum. The permission was granted, as long as she stayed under guard. Once she arrived,

CREATE AN EGYPTIAN-STYLE NECKLACE

As was the case with most queens, Cleopatra had plenty of jewelry from different parts of the world. Colorful necklaces that covered the upper chest were favorites among Egyptians. Some were so heavy that the wearer had to hang a heavy jewel on the back as a counterweight. Others, like the one in this activity, were simpler.

MATERIALS

- Scissors
- Strong thread that fits through your beads
- Pipe cleaner
- 250 multicolor beads

1. Cut five 18-inch pieces of strong thread.

2. Tie the first piece of thread to one end of a pipe cleaner.

3. Take the free end of the thread and string multicolored beads onto it. You may string them freely or create a pattern. Stop about 2 inches from the end of the string.

4. Tie the free end of the thread to the other end of the pipe cleaner.

5. Bend the tips of the pipe cleaner to secure the string.

6. Tie one end of another piece of thread to the pipe cleaner next to the first string of beads (closer to the center of the pipe cleaner).

7. Repeat steps 3 and 4 with this string, but use two to three fewer beads. Tie the other end of the second thread near the other end of the first (closer to the center of the pipe cleaner). Lay the necklace on a flat surface to make sure the second line of beads lies neatly above the first and doesn't overlap it. If it does overlap, you will need to untie one end of the second thread, remove one or more beads, and tie it shorter.

8. Repeat steps 6 and 7 with other pieces of string. You may string as many as five rows of beads (no more, or it might not fit over your head).

9. Cut off any excess string from the ends. Wear your necklace proudly!

she delivered a dramatic speech to her dead lover, expressing her pain at being separated from him in death: Antony, the Roman, would stay in Alexandria, while the queen of Egypt would end her days in Italy. "The gods of this country have betrayed us," she mournfully admitted. Could Antony's gods help? She had only one request: to be spared the humiliation of the Roman triumph and be buried next to her lover.

After returning to her room, she bathed, dressed in her finest clothes, and ate with her

maids. She then asked her guard to deliver to Octavian a writing tablet imprinted with a message.

The message repeated the same appeal: she wanted to be buried with Antony. Octavian understood the hidden meaning. She was no longer begging for her life. He rushed to the palace, but it was too late. Cleopatra lay on a golden couch, dead. Her maid Iras was dead at her side, and Charmion, dying by Cleopatra's head, made one last attempt to arrange the queen's crown.

Octavian ordered a search for the suicide weapon, but no one could find it. The only clue were some puncture marks on her arm. He assumed she had smuggled a poisonous snake into the room and sent for some Libyan snake charmers to suck out the poison. It was useless.

It was August 12, 30 BC. Cleopatra was about 40 years old, a ripe age at a time of limited medical care, and had successfully ruled Egypt for 22 years.

The Legend of the Asp

As it is written, the snake story is unconvincing. First, it would have taken more than one to kill three women. And how could multiple snakes be smuggled into a room under high surveillance—especially large poisonous snakes like the Egyptian asp or cobra? Also snakebite poisoning usually causes great discomfort, and even convulsions, over hours, and Charmion, who was seconds away from dying, didn't seem to be in any terrible pain.

Besides, death by snake is not a foolproof method. Sometimes snakes refuse to bite, and sometimes the poison is not effective. Cleopatra wouldn't have risked a failed attempt. More important, where did the snake go afterward? No one could find it, either in the room or outside Cleopatra's window. Some suggested a more practical possibility: a pin smeared or filled with poison—or three pins, one per woman—and hidden in her hair.

The only way the snake story makes sense is if Cleopatra wanted to use an instrument of death that had a strong symbolic meaning in Egypt, and if Octavian's security measures were less strict than what early historians have claimed they were. That could very well have been the case. After all, Octavian had everything to gain from Cleopatra's suicide, as it allowed him to show himself as a merciful ruler who had done everything possible to keep her alive. According to Plutarch, the young man who told her about Octavian's timetable felt "a certain tenderness for Cleopatra." Others wonder, however, if he had been sent by Octavian to drive her to suicide.

In the end, it's safest to conclude, like Dio, that "no one knows clearly in what way she perished." What we know is that she was finally entombed next to Antony, just as she had wished.

Octavian's Takeover

"Now it's time to drink!" cheered Horace. Like many others, he celebrated the Roman conquest of Egypt as the end of years of civil wars and violence that had characterized the previous century. At 33 years old, Octavian had unchallenged authority over the Mediterranean world. Some hailed him as the new Alexander the Great, who had died at age 33.

Octavian stayed in Egypt six months to oversee the change of administration, strengthen the Roman troops, and plan improved methods of irrigation. He allowed the completion of Cleopatra's mausoleum according to her plans but ordered the destruction of all images of Antony. He would have done the same for images of Cleopatra, but one of her friends paid 1,000 talents to protect them. Only a few survive today.

Octavian could certainly use the 1,000 talents, as well as the many riches he collected from Cleopatra, to pay his veterans and make improvements in Rome. In a way, Cleopatra had made it easy for him, because she had gathered a lot of money and treasures for her planned escape. He also took an abundance of trophies to display in Rome, including two giant obelisks that are still standing today.

What Came Next

In the end, Cleopatra didn't completely escape the humiliation she feared. Both a statue and a painting of her (holding a snake in her final moments) were taken in triumph through the streets of Rome, followed by her three youngest children, all in chains. Alexander Helios and Cleopatra Selene were about 11 years old, and Ptolemy Philadelphus was about 7. Due to their ages, they were allowed to live under the care of Octavia, who became the official mother of all of Antony's children.

Originally built in Heliopolis, Egypt, by Pharaohs Seti I and Ramses II (around 1200 BC), Octavian brought the Flaminio Obelisk to Rome in 10 BC as a commemoration of his victory over Egypt. *Nuno Vilela, Flickr*

Things didn't go well for Caesarion and Antyllus, who had both become men and couldn't be trusted. Both young men were deceived by their tutors. Caesarion's tutor persuaded him to abandon a trip to India and return to Alexandria, convincing him that Octavian would be lenient. As soon as Caesarion arrived, Octavian ordered his death. Antyllus's tutor had an eye on a jewel the boy carried under his tunic and betrayed him to the Romans in order to get it. After a pointless resistance, Antyllus was captured and beheaded on Octavian's orders. His tutor grabbed the jewel but was discovered and executed for theft.

Cleopatra Selene went on to marry King Juba II of Numidia, Juba I's only child, who had walked in chains as a boy alongside Arsinoe during Caesar's 46 BC triumph. Since then, Juba had been raised as a Roman citizen and had become an officer in Rome's army and a good friend of Octavian. He was also famous as a poet, historian, and geographer. Cleopatra Selene, who had started her education under one of the finest scholars in Alexandria, had much in common with her husband.

In 25 BC, Juba and Cleopatra Selene went to govern Mauretania (an area including modern Algeria and northern Morocco) under Rome's supervision.

TRANSPORT AN OBELISK ON WATER

Obelisks were usually made of red granite and could be as tall as 100 feet. Transporting them across the country (and later overseas) was quite a feat. They were first placed on a heavy sled and dragged on sand to the river, then mounted on boats.

An Egyptian painting shows a person moistening the sand before a sled was pulled over it. The right quantity of water makes the sand firmer and prevents it from piling up in front of the sled. (Try dragging a heavy object on dry sand and on wet sand and see the difference.)

When the obelisk reached the river, it was probably laid across it, while a boat carrying equally heavy cargo arrived underneath. At that point, the cargo was removed and the boat would rise to lift the obelisk and carry it down the river.

You can test this principle by using materials you may have around the home.

MATERIALS

- 7-by-12-by-3-inch clear storage container
- Water
- 12-inch skewer, ruler, or stick
- 1-ounce box of raisins
- Small plastic container

1. Fill a 7-by-12-by-3-inch clear storage container halfway with water and lay a 12-inch skewer, ruler, or stick evenly across the top of the container.

2. Place a 1-ounce box of raisins in the center of a small plastic container, then place the small container in the water at one end of the large container so that it floats. Adjust the box of raisins if needed.

3. Gently guide the small container to float under the center of the skewer.

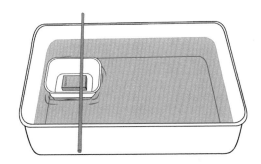

4. Holding the small container in place, remove the box of raisins.

5. Let go of the small container and watch it as it rises and lifts the skewer.

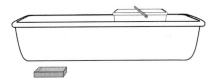

6. Gently push the small container, with the skewer on top of it, to the other end of the large container. Obelisks were obviously heavier than your skewer, but the boats were also larger and stronger than your container. This activity can give you a general idea of how the ancients transported obelisks along rivers and even across oceans.

They called their first son Ptolemy, a continuation of Cleopatra's lineage. During Cleopatra Selene's reign, she kept both her Greek and Egyptian heritage by promoting Greco-Roman culture in the capital city and issuing Egyptian-style coins depicting Isis, crocodiles, and religious Egyptian instruments. There is no clear record of the lives of Alexander Helios and Ptolemy Philadelphus, but Dio wrote that they moved into their sister's royal court.

French actress Sarah Bernhardt's portrayal of Cleopatra in an 1890 play.
Library of Congress

One is left to wonder what might have been had Cleopatra gone to Rome and suffered her temporary humiliation next to her children in Octavian's triumphal parade. If she had retired in exile like her sister had done, she would have received news of her children and their accomplishments or might have been allowed to live with them. But ordinary stories don't make news, and she might not have been permanently impressed in the imagination of so many.

Survival

Cleopatra's death marked the Roman takeover of Egypt—a takeover against which she had fought with all her might—and the end of Egypt's independence. The regime change, however, didn't disrupt the majority of Egyptians' lives along the banks of the Nile. Regardless of who was in charge, they worked the land, paid taxes, and sacrificed to the gods in hope of receiving health and prosperity. In fact, the Egyptian priests worked hard to keep a feeling of continuity by depicting each ruler in typical pharaoh's garb, performing the same sacrifices to the gods. It didn't matter if the rulers despised those gods (as Octavian did). As long as the people could believe in a continuation of peace and order, the *maat* was not interrupted.

At the same time, Egyptian culture became very fashionable in Rome, and Egyptian antiquities started to embellish the houses of the rich and famous. It was the first bout of a phenomenon known as Egyptomania, which returned at different times in history, particularly in the 1800s, when hieroglyphs were finally interpreted.

Of all the Egyptian tales, Cleopatra's story, in its different variations, has been one of the most enduring. Today most people know her only as the beautiful enchantress portrayed in movies. Few remember how she struggled to lead her country during two of the most turbulent decades in world history and how, unlike her father, she managed to meet Rome's constant demands without incurring debts or causing major insurrections.

Unfortunately most primary sources are lost and much of her story is unknown. As historian Peter Green wrote:

Enigmatic? Oh sure, she beats the Mona
Lisa at that game. Which is why we can't resist
reinventing her in our own image. . . .
But the heart eludes
our searching: her childish dreams, her taste
*   in wines,*
her jokes, her favorite scents, her kitchen feuds,
the losses that made her cry, portents and
*   signs*
that moved her. All we know is the queen,
take her or leave her. A mystery. What it meant
is your guess or mine, forever.

ACKNOWLEDGMENTS

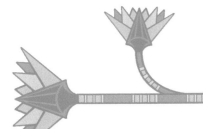

As with all my books, I am deeply touched by the kindness and generosity of those who have helped to make this volume a reality. Once more, I thank my editor, Lisa Reardon, who helped me decide in favor of this fascinating subject, and all the staff at Chicago Review Press. I also want to thank my great host of friends and encouragers who have given me convincing reasons I should tackle a task that seemed monumental, especially Nancy Sanders, Rebecca Richards, Rev. Michael Brown, Glenda Mathes, Janie Cheaney, and my husband, Tom.

I thank all those who have thoughtfully taken the time to read some of my early drafts, including screenwriter Dianna Ippolito; editors Heather Chisholm-Chait, Robin Witkin, and Timothy Massaro; and author and artist Troy Howell. I am especially indebted to Dr. Adrian Goldsworthy, author of *Antony and Cleopatra*, and Dr. Joyce Tyldesley, author of *Cleopatra: Last Queen of Egypt*, for answering my numerous questions and giving me recommendations; to blogger Gawhara Hanem for helping me explore interesting questions about Cleopatra; and to Dr. Shelley P. Haley, professor of classics and Africana studies at Hamilton College, for taking the time to read my sidebar on Cleopatra's race and give suggestions on how best to explain the puzzling issue.

GLOSSARY

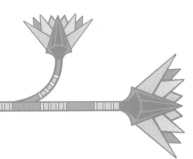

agora A marketplace and gathering spot in ancient Greece.

alchemist Someone who studies an early form of chemistry practiced in medieval times, mostly based on the transformation of matter.

archaeology The study of ancient civilizations by searching for and examining their monuments, tools, and other objects.

bust A sculpture representing only the head and shoulders of a person.

capital In architecture, the top part of a column.

cartouche An oval containing the name of a king or queen in Egyptian hieroglyphs.

cartridge A metal container that holds an explosive charge or bullet.

client ruler The ruler of a state who manages his or her own administration under the strict control of a more powerful state.

consul The highest elected political office in the Roman republic. Consuls stayed in office for one year. If the Senate decided to extend a consul's power, the consul was known as a proconsul.

cornucopia A horn-shaped container, usually filled with fruits and flowers; a symbol of abundance.

court The residence of a king, queen, or other ruler who is a member of the nobility.

cremation The disposition of a dead body by reducing it to ashes.

Cupid In Roman mythology, a messenger of love, son of the gods Mercury and Venus.

defect To abandon an army or a cause to join another.

delta The fan-shaped portion of land at the mouth of a river.

dictator A ruler who holds total power. In the Roman republic, a man could be appointed dictator for six months in times of crisis.

dynasty A succession of rulers belonging to the same family.

Egyptologist An archaeologist who specializes in the study of ancient Egypt.

embalming Preserving a dead body—with spices in ancient times, with chemicals in modern times.

frankincense African tree resin that is burned as incense or used in essential oils.

Hellenistic Belonging to the Greek culture that spread throughout the Mediterranean.

hieroglyph A character used in hieroglyphic writing.

hieroglyphic A written language whose characters are mostly pictures.

imperator In the early Roman Republic, this was a general title given to a magistrate who held military command. In the late republic, it became an honorary title for winning commanders. During the empire, it was used for the emperor.

irrigation The process of watering land by artificial means.

legion Basic military unit of the Roman army of about 5,000 men.

lever A bar resting on a support (or fulcrum) and used to lift heavy objects with one end by placing pressure on the other.

litter A chair, couch, or bed carried on poles by servants known as bearers.

mausoleum A large tomb.

mercenary A soldier hired by a foreign country to fight in exchange for money.

mooring Fastening a ship or boat in place using ropes or anchors.

mummification The process of drying and bandaging a dead body.

mummy A body preserved for burial through a drying and bandaging process.

myrrh An African or Arabian tree resin that is burned as incense or used in perfumes and medicines.

nymph In ancient mythology, one of the young goddesses living in mountains, forests, meadows, and waters.

obelisk A tall, narrow, four-sided monument that tapers off into a pyramid at the top.

omen An event that is considered a sign or warning of things to come.

papyrus A tall reed that grows abundantly by the Nile River; also the writing material derived from the central part of papyrus stems.

parchment Ancient writing material made from the skin of a sheep or goat.

pharaoh Ancient Egypt's supreme ruler.

proconsul A Roman consul whose power is extended for longer than a year.

promontory A large portion of land that sticks out into the sea.

propaganda Information that is spread in order to influence public opinion.

province In ancient times, the basic unit of Rome's possessions outside of Italy.

relief A sculpture on which the design is raised from the background.

republic A type of government in which the supreme power is held by citizens or their representatives rather than a single ruler.

scholar A specialist in a branch of study.

scribe A person trained in writing and copying documents.

Senate The supreme ruling council of the ancient Roman republic.

sesterces A Roman coin. Ten sesterces could buy about four pounds of bread or a medium-sized meal in Rome during Cleopatra's life.

shaft In architecture, the stem of a column.

signet ring A ring with initials or a design that was used as a stamp on official documents.

sphinx A mythological beast with the body of a lion and the head of a man, ram, or bird.

stela A slab of stone or a column bearing an inscription or design to commemorate an event.

stern The rear part of a boat.

talent Greek and Roman measurement of weight and (as a result) of money.

toga The loose outer garment worn in public by citizens of ancient Rome.

triumvirate A political group of three people.

vanguard The troops that move ahead of an army.

TIME LINE OF EGYPTIAN DYNASTIES

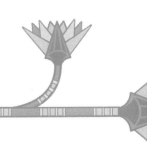

(All dates are BC. Most are approximate.)

3050–2686 | **Dynasties 1–2—Early Dynasties**

Main events: King Narmer unifies Egypt, establishing his capital in Memphis, a few miles south of today's Cairo.

2686–2181 | **Dynasties 3–6—Old Kingdom**

Main events: The age of the pyramids—from the Step Pyramid of Saqqâra to the Pyramid of Kahfre.

2181–2055 | **Dynasties 7–11—First Intermediate Period**

Main events: With the fall of a central authority, Egypt divides into independent communities. Gradually, two dynasties emerge.

2055–1650 | **Dynasties 11–13—Middle Kingdom**

Main events: Mentuhotep II of Thebes reunites Egypt and brings political stability. The Egyptians conquer northern Nubia. A series of weak kings brings an end to the Middle Kingdom.

1650–1550 | **Dynasties 14–17—Second Intermediate Period**

Main events: The Hyksos, a population of Asian settlers, rise to power and rule northern Egypt from the delta city of Avaris. The Theban kings fight to reunite Egypt.

1550–1069 | **Dynasties 18–20—New Kingdom**

Main events: The Theban king Ahmose expels the Hyksos, chasing them into Canaan. The 18th Dynasty kings expand Egypt to cover territories from the Sudan to Syria. They also stop building pyramids and carve tombs into the Valley of the Kings. It is an age of famous kings such as Hatshepsut (the "female king"), Akhenaten and Nefertiti (an unconventional royal couple who promote the worship of only one god and move the capital to Amarna), Tutankhamen (the "boy king"), and Ramses II. After Ramses II, the country becomes progressively weaker until it divides again.

1069–664 | **Dynasties 21–25—Third Intermediate Period**

A period of gradual decay, culminating with an invasion by the Assyrians, who set up a puppet king under their rule: Necho I.

664–332 | **Dynasties 26–31—Late Period**

Necho's son Psamtik reunites the land under his rule. A time of peace and cultural renewal until in 525 the Persians invade Egypt, setting up governors in the land.

332–30 | **Ptolemaic Dynasty**

Alexander the Great conquers Egypt in 332 BC. In 331 BC he founds Alexandria. He dies in 323 BCE, and his general Ptolemy I takes over Egypt. The death of the last Ptolemy, Cleopatra VII, in 30 BC marks the end of the Egyptian dynasties, as Egypt becomes part of the Roman Empire.

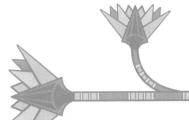

RESOURCES TO EXPLORE

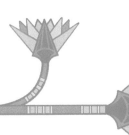

BOOKS

Brier, Bob. *Cleopatra's Needles: The Lost Obelisks of Egypt.* **London: Bloomsbury Academic, 2016.**
Grades 4–12. Though not written for children, this book is simple and accessible to young readers. It tells the fascinating and often adventurous story of the construction and transportation of obelisks in Egypt and around the world.

Broida, Marian. *Ancient Egyptians and Their Neighbors: An Activity Guide.* **Chicago: Chicago Review Press, 1999.**
Grades 4–8. Forty activities and much interesting information covering the civilizations around Egypt that are often neglected in schoolbooks.

Giblin, James Cross. *The Riddle of the Rosetta Stone: Key to Ancient Egypt.* **New York: HarperTrophy, 1990.**
Grades 3–8. The interesting story of the Rosetta Stone and how hieroglyphs began to be deciphered.

Giblin, James Cross. *Secrets of the Sphinx.* **New York: Scholastic, 2004.**
Grades 4–8. Interesting facts about the Egyptian Sphinx.

McDonald, Angela. *Write Your Own Egyptian Hieroglyphs: Names, Greetings, Insults, Sayings.* **Berkeley: University of California Press, 2007.**
Grades 3–8. An interesting and fun book for anyone interested in beginning to read and write hieroglyphs.

Millimore, Mark. *Imagining Egypt: A Living Portrait of the Time of the Pharaohs.* New York: Black Dog & Leventhal, 2007.

Grades 4–12. Not written specifically for children, it will delight readers of all ages with its highly illustrated, colorful pages and comprehensive contents.

Tyldesley, Joyce. *Egypt.* New York: Simon & Schuster, 2007.

Grades 3–7. This might be the best overview for children of Ancient Egyptian life and customs.

MUSEUMS TO VISIT IN PERSON OR ONLINE

British Museum
London, England
www.britishmuseum.org/learning/schools_and_teachers/resources/cultures/ancient_egypt.aspx

Resources for teachers and parents with recommended books, interactive sites, activities, and more. If you are able to visit in person, this museum holds over 100,000 Egyptian archaeological objects.

Grand Egyptian Museum
Giza, Egypt
Alexandria Desert Road, Kafr Nassar, Al Haram, Giza Governorate

If you are visiting Egypt, don't miss this collection of over 100,000 objects.

Kelsey Museum of Archaeology
Ann Arbor, Michigan
https://lsa.umich.edu/kelsey/education/k-12-educators-and-schools.html

Includes many Egyptian artifacts, including a large collection of mummy masks. Besides offering tours, experts from the museum are available for school presentations.

Metropolitan Museum of Art
New York, New York
www.metmuseum.org

Holds 26,000 pieces of Egyptian art, especially from the Middle Kingdom and early New Kingdom, and provides guided tours.

Museum of Fine Arts, Boston
Boston, Massachusetts
www.mfa.org/node/9457

One of the most important collections of Egyptian artifacts in the world. Their website includes an interesting virtual tour.

National Museums of Scotland
Edinburgh, Scotland
www.nms.ac.uk/explore/games/discover-ancient-egypt

Holds around 6,000 objects from Ancient Egypt, including sculptures, mummies, papyri, furniture, and jewelry. Fun, interactive online games.

Oriental Institute
Chicago, Illinois
https://oi.uchicago.edu

Offers guided tours and fun family events to help children understand ancient Egyptian culture.

Petrie Museum
London, England
www.ucl.ac.uk/culture/petrie-museum

One of the largest collections of Egyptian and Sudanese archeology in the world (about 80,000 objects).

The Walters Art Museum
Baltimore, Maryland
http://art.thewalters.org/browse/category/ancient-egypt-and-nubia
https://thewalters.org/pachydermpubs/mummified

An interesting collection of Egyptian and Nubian artifacts. The museum also provides an interactive online exhibit exploring the art of mummification.

WEBSITES

BBC Ancient History—Egypt
www.bbc.co.uk/history/ancient/egyptians

Interesting information and interactive games.

Build Your Own New York—Cleopatra's Needle

www.buildyourownnewyork.com/Cleopatra.pdf

Interesting information on the New York obelisk, a transcription of its hieroglyphs, and instructions on how to build a cardboard obelisk.

Children's University of Manchester

www.childrensuniversity.manchester.ac.uk/interactives/history/egypt

Website with interesting facts, activities, and interactive games.

Discovering Egypt

https://discoveringegypt.com

The unique character of this website is in its computer-generated reconstructions of ancient Egyptian buildings and cities. There is also a treasure of information.

NOVA—Explore Ancient Egypt

www.pbs.org/wgbh/nova/ancient/explore-ancient-egypt.html

An interactive tour of ancient Egypt.

WikiHow—How to Make Papyrus

www.wikihow.com/Make-Papyrus

An illustrated explanation of how papyrus sheets were made, plus an activity that mimics the same technique.

VIDEOS

Cleopatra's "Coin" Hairstyle: Exploration and Recreation

www.youtube.com/watch?v=Trp9S5AlmeQ

Instructions on how to recreate Cleopatra's hairstyle by Janet Stephens, a professional stylist and amateur archaeologist who specializes in ancient and historic hairdressing.

Egypt According to Cleopatra

www.youtube.com/watch?v=X92qU7CWurI

An interesting, short documentary in three parts, showing many monuments, including a reconstruction of ancient Alexandria and the Alexandrian lighthouse.

NOTES

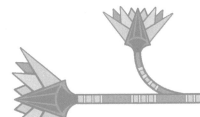
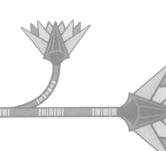

Chapter 1: A Young Princess of an Ancient Land

"to the strongest": Diodorus Siculus, *The Library of History*, vol. 8, Loeb Classical Library (Cambridge, MA: Harvard University Press, 1963), 17.117.3, http://penelope.uchicago.edu/Thayer/E/Roman/Texts/Diodorus_Siculus/17F*.html

"pass from one language to another": Plutarch, *The Parallel Lives*, trans. Bernadotte Perrin, vol. 9, *The Life of Antony*, Loeb Classical Library (Cambridge, MA: Harvard University Press, 1920), 27.3, http://penelope.uchicago.edu/Thayer/E/Roman/Texts/Plutarch/Lives/Antony*.html.

"eldest daughter of the king": Joyce Tyldesley, *Cleopatra: Last Queen of Egypt* (New York: Basic Books, 2008), 39.

Chapter 2: The Fight for the Throne

"settle their disputes": Julius Caesar, *The Civil Wars*, trans. Arthur George Peskett, Loeb Classical Library (Cambridge, MA: Harvard University Press, 1914), 107, http://penelope.uchicago.edu/Thayer/E/Roman/Texts/Caesar/Civil_Wars/3D*.html.

"inside a bed-sack" . . . *"with a cord"*: Plutarch, *The Parallel Lives*, trans. Bernadotte Perrin, vol. 7, *The Life of Julius Caesar*, Loeb Classical Library (Cambridge, MA: Harvard University Press, 1919), 49.2, http://penelope.uchicago.edu/Thayer/e/roman/texts/plutarch/lives/caesar*.html.

"was in itself": Plutarch, *Parallel Lives: Antony*, 27.2.

"a combination of frankincense": Bob Brier and Hoyt Hobbes, *Ancient Egypt: Everyday Life in the Land of the Nile* (New York: Sterling, 2009), 264.

"a work of wonderful construction": Caesar, *Civil Wars*, 112.

"If they proved ungrateful": Julius Caesar, *The Alexandrian War*, trans. A. G. Way, Loeb Classical Library, (Cambridge, MA: Harvard University Press, 1955), 33.27, http://penelope.uchicago.edu/Thayer/E/Roman/Texts/Caesar/Alexandrian_War/A*.html.

Chapter 3: Cleopatra's Cruise

"exploring the country": Appian, *The Roman History*, trans. Horace White, vol. 4, *The Civil Wars*, Loeb Classical Library (Cambridge, MA: Harvard University Press, 1913), 2.90, http://penelope.uchicago.edu/Thayer/e/roman/texts/appian/civil_wars/5*.html.

"The Egyptians have a climate": Herodotus, *Histories*, trans. A. D. Godley (Cambridge, MA: Harvard University Press), 1920, 2.35.2, www.perseus.tufts.edu/hopper/text?doc=Perseus:text:1999.01.0126.

"the most wonders": Herodotus, 2.35.1.

"gazing out over the ocean of Time": Mark Twain, *The Innocents Abroad: Roughing It* (New York: Library of America, 1984), 502.

"his soldiers refused to follow him": Gaius Suetonius Tranquillus, *The Lives of the Twelve Caesars*, trans. J. C. Rolfe, Loeb Classical Library (Cambridge, MA: Harvard University Press: 1913–1914), 1.52.1, http://penelope.uchicago.edu/Thayer/E/Roman/Texts/Suetonius/12Caesars/home.html.

Chapter 4: The New Goddess Isis

"[Caesar] incurred": Cassius Dio, *Roman History*, trans. Earnest Cary, vol. 4, Loeb Classical Library. (Cambridge, MA: Harvard University Press, 1914–1927), 43.27.3, http://penelope.uchicago.edu/Thayer/e/roman/texts/cassius_dio/home.html.

"was not at all concerned": Dio, 43.27.3.

"with or without Ptolemy": Tyldesley, *Cleopatra*, 106.

"You too, my child?": Suetonius, *Twelve Caesars*, 1.82.2.

"She was also by nature": Flavius Josephus, *Antiquities of the Jews*, trans. William Whiston, 15.4.1.88, www.perseus.tufts.edu/hopper/text?doc=Perseus:text:1999.01.0146.

Chapter 5: Cleopatra and Mark Antony

"be afraid of Antony": Plutarch, *Parallel Lives: Antony*, 25.2.

"decked out in fine array": Homer, *Iliad*, 14.162, quoted in Plutarch, *Parallel Lives: Antony*, 25.2.

"for the good of Asia": Plutarch, 26.3.

"Dionysus Giver of Joy": Plutarch, 24.3.

"multitude of lights": Plutarch, 26.4.

"Imperator": Plutarch, 29.4.

Chapter 6: Queen of Kings

"to draw Antony away": Plutarch, *Parallel Lives: Antony*, 30.2.

"Antony's reproaches": Appian, *Roman History*, 6.59.

"took no thought for spinning": Plutarch, *Parallel Lives: Antony*, 10.3.

"a wonder of a woman": Plutarch, 31.1.

"Year 16 that is Year 1": Tyldesley, *Cleopatra*, 163.

"beside himself with distress": Plutarch, *Parallel Lives: Antony*, 51.1.

"I shall not leave him": "New Kingdom Song," quoted in Joyce Tyldesley, *Daughters of Isis: Women of Ancient Egypt* (London: Penguin Books, 1994), 56.

"My heart thought": Miriam Lichtheim, *Ancient Egyptian Literature*, vol. 2, *The New Kingdom* (Berkeley: University of California Press, 2006), 191.

"Queen of Kings" . . . *"King of Kings"*: Tyldesley, *Cleopatra*, 168.

"An Alexandrian crowd collected": C. P. Cavafy, "Alexandrian Kings," trans. George Valassopoulo, in E. M. Forster, *Pharos and Pharillon* (Surrey, UK: Hogarth, 1923), 78–79.

Chapter 7: The Sharers of Death

"Why have you changed?": Gaius Suetonius Tranquillus, *De Vita XII Caesarum*, Loeb Classical Library (Cambridge, MA: Harvard University Press: 1913), 2.69.1 (my translation), http://penelope.uchicago.edu/Thayer/L/Roman/Texts/Suetonius/12Caesars/Augustus*.html.

"Octavia and Athena": Seneca the Elder, *Suasoriae*, 1.6 (my translation), www.perseus.tufts.edu/hopper/text?doc=Perseus%3Atext%3A2008.01.0562.

"All Italy": Augustus, *The Deeds of the Divine Augustus*, trans. Thomas Bushnell (self-pub: 1998), 25, http://classics.mit.edu/Augustus/deeds.html.

"see how Cleopatra": Plutarch, *Parallel Lives: Antony*, 56.3.

"one of the biggest and boldest": Toby Wilkinson, *The Rise and Fall of Ancient Egypt* (London: Bloomsbury, 2011), 506.

"Look, Mark Antony": Pliny the Elder, *Natural History*, 21.9 (my translation), http://penelope.uchicago.edu/Thayer/L/Roman/Texts/Pliny_the_Elder/21*.html.

"filled Antony with fears": Dio, *Roman History*, 50.3.3.

"in silence": Plutarch, *Parallel Lives: Antony*, 67.1.

"the enjoyment of suppers": Plutarch, 71.2.

Chapter 8: The End of an Era

"came poor": Plutarch, *Parallel Lives: Antony*, 73.3.

"When at the hour of midnight": C. P. Cavafy, *The God Abandons Antony*, trans. George Valassopoulo, in E. M. Forster, *Pharos and Pharillon* (Surrey, UK: Hogarth, 1923), 46.

"Smeared with blood and struggling": Plutarch, *Parallel Lives: Antony*, 77.2.

"master, husband, and imperator": Plutarch, 77.3.

"Wretched Cleopatra, you are taken alive": Plutarch, 79.2 (my translation).

"the gentlest of commanders": Plutarch, 79.2.

"the most agreeable": Plutarch, 25.2.

"not a humble woman": Horace, *Carminum*, 1.37.30 (my translation), www.the latinlibrary.com/horace/carm1.shtml.

"The gods of this country": Plutarch, *Parallel Lives: Antony*, 84.4.

"a certain tenderness": Plutarch, 84.1.

"no one knows": Dio, *Roman History*, 51.14.1.

"Now it's time to drink!": Horace, *Carminum*, 1.37.1 (my translation).

"Enigmatic? Oh sure": Peter Green, "Epilogue. Cleopatra: The Sphynx Revisited," in *Cleopatra: A Sphinx Revisited*, ed. Margaret M. Miles (Berkeley: University of California Press, 2011), 212.

SELECTED BIBLIOGRAPHY

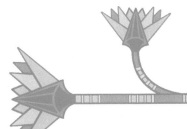
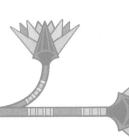

Classical Sources

Appian. *The Roman History: The Civil Wars*. Vols. 1–3.26. Translated by Horace White. Loeb Classical Library. Cambridge, MA: Harvard University Press, 1913. http://penelope.uchicago.edu/Thayer/e/roman/texts/appian/civil_wars/5*.html.

Caesar, Julius. *The Alexandrian War*. Translated by A. G. Way. Loeb Classical Library. Cambridge, MA: Harvard University Press: 1955. http://penelope.uchicago.edu/Thayer/E/Roman/Texts/Caesar/Alexandrian_War/A*.html.

Caesar, Julius. *The Civil Wars*. Translated by Arthur George Peskett. Loeb Classical Library. Cambridge, MA: Harvard University Press, 1914. http://penelope.uchicago.edu/Thayer/E/Roman/Texts/Caesar/Civil_Wars/3D*.html.

Dio, Cassius. *Roman History*. Translated by Earnest Cary. 9 vols. Loeb Classical Library. Cambridge, MA: Harvard University Press, 1914–1927. http://penelope.uchicago.edu/Thayer/e/roman/texts/cassius_dio/home.html.

Herodotus. *Histories*. Vol. 2. Translated by A. D. Godley. Cambridge, MA: Harvard University Press, 1920. www.perseus.tufts.edu/hopper/text?doc=Perseus:text:1999.01.0126.

Plutarch. *The Parallel Lives*. Translated by Bernadotte Perrin. Vol. 7, *The Life of Julius Caesar*. Loeb Classical Library. Cambridge, MA: Harvard University Press, 1919. http://penelope.uchicago.edu/Thayer/e/roman/texts/plutarch/lives/caesar*.html.

Plutarch. *The Parallel Lives*. Translated by Bernadotte Perrin. Vol. 9, *The Life of Antony*. Loeb Classical Library. Cambridge, MA: Harvard University Press, 1920. http://penelope.uchicago.edu/Thayer/E/Roman/Texts/Plutarch/Lives/Antony*.html.

Suetonius Tranquillus, Gaius. *The Lives of the Twelve Caesars*. Vol. 1. Translated by J. C. Rolfe. Loeb Classical Library. Cambridge, MA: Harvard University Press: 1913–1914. http://penelope.uchicago.edu/Thayer/E/Roman/Texts/Suetonius/12Caesars/home.html.

Modern Texts

Brier, Bob, and Hoyt Hobbes. *Ancient Egypt: Everyday Life in the Land of the Nile*. New York: Sterling, 2009.

Goldsworthy, Adrian. *Antony and Cleopatra*. New Haven, CT: Yale University Press, 2010.

Jones, Prudence. J. *Cleopatra: A Sourcebook*. Norman: University of Oklahoma Press, 1971.

Tyldesley, Joyce. *Cleopatra: Last Queen of Egypt*. New York: Basic Books, 2008.

INDEX

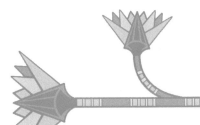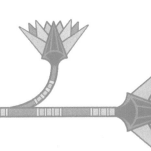